The Fellowship Movement

The Fellowship Movement

A Growth Strategy and Its Legacy

Holley Ulbrich

SKINNER HOUSE BOOKS
BOSTON

 Published by Skinner House Books, an imprint of the Unitarian Universalist Association of Congregations, a liberal religious organization with more than 1,000 congregations in the U.S. and Canada. 25 Beacon St., Boston, MA 02108-2800.

Printed in the United States.

Cover and Text design by Suzanne Morgan
Cover photo courtesy of the UUA archives.

ISBN 1 55896-530-0
978-1-55896-530-0

6 5 4 3 2 1
10 09 08 07

Library of Congress Cataloging-in-Publication Data

Ulbrich, Holley H.
The fellowship movement : a growth strategy and its legacy / Holley Ulbrich.
p. cm.
Includes bibliographical references and index.
ISBN-13: 978-1-55896-530-0 (pbk. : alk. paper)
ISBN-10: 1-55896-530-0 (pbk. : alk. paper) 1. Unitarian Universalist Association—History. 2. Fellowship--Religious aspects—Unitarian Universalist churches. I. Title.

BX9833.U43 2007
289.1'32—dc22

2007031471

Contents

Introduction

The growth of Unitarian Universalism in the last 60 years is largely the story of the fellowship movement and its aftermath.

Between 1948 and 1967, the main growth strategy of the American Unitarian Association (AUA) and its successor, the Unitarian Universalist Association (UUA), was to plant small, autonomous, lay-led congregations just about everywhere ten or more religious liberals could be brought together. While the Universalists tried creating house churches in the South in the late 19th century, and even a few lay-led congregations in the 1950s, this large-scale experiment in church growth was both unique in the American religious landscape and controversial.

The Fellowship Movement is a retrospective on 20 years that shaped the course of Unitarian Universalism in the last half century, as well as an overview of what has become of the "first-wave" fellowships (those born during that period). I hope it will offer some insight into how these pioneer settlements and their frontier brand of religion have shaped present-day Unitarian Universalism —including the way congregations perceive themselves and are perceived by outsiders, the style of Unitarian Universalist worship, and the role of laypersons in all aspects of congregational life.

As a faith tradition without commonly agreed-upon scriptures, divine revelation, or official creed, Unitarian Universalism is bound together primarily by shared values and a shared history. Thus, the history of the fellowship movement is an essential part of our identity. There have been two earlier efforts to bring this history to light: Laile Bartlett's *Bright Galaxy* in 1960 and a heavily researched and lengthy sermon by the late Rev. Dan O'Neal, "In Fellowship We Trust," in 1994.

Now, 40 years after the end of the fellowship movement, we can take a new, thoughtful look backward while we still have surviving founders of these fellowships to share the rich oral history of their congregations. The story of the fellowship movement deserves to be retold in some detail, replete with regional nuances and the creation, growth, and death stories that lie behind the statistics.

Although official support for the fellowship movement as a growth strategy ended in 1967, lay-led fellowships are still the primary model for new Unitarian Universalist congregations. These congregations, brought to life by determined groups of religious liberals, can grow into full-fledged churches or remain small and isolated, depending on how we as a religious movement choose to set our priorities and allocate our scarce resources. Thus, the story of the fellowship movement is not only about the growth of Unitarian Universalism in the last 60 years; it is also the story of our future.

A note on terminology is in order. The congregations described in this book are most often referred to as *fellowships*, because that is the name they generally used themselves. That name tended to stick even after they had grown into a more traditional religious community (if they did), complete with building, minister and religious education program. The American Unitarian Association insisted on distinguishing between fellowship and church in the 1950s, calling the congregation a *church* when it reached a certain size and had a minister. (This insistence did not necessarily lead to a congregation changing its name in every case.) The choice of the right word to use was and remains problematic for many of our congregations, with the word *congregation* being the least controversial choice. *Church* sounds too Christian for many members who either do not come from a Christian background or are running away from it. *Society* may sound too formal. In this volume, I use the word *church* when the congregation itself has chosen that name or when I am making a distinction between congregations birthed as fellowships and those originating either before the fellowship period or by a different route—such as a new start, complete with a minister financed by the AUA or UUA.

In light of the separation between the Canadian and U.S. denominational associations, this book addresses only congregations in the United States, although the fellowship movement played an important role in Canada as well. During site visits to some 20 congregations in 13 states, my collaborators (Rev. Cynthia Prescott and my husband Carlton) and I met with ministers, small groups, and a number of district executives. Information from these conversations was supplemented with individual interviews, email correspondence, research at the Andover-Harvard Theological Library archives, countless telephone conversations, and intensive study of congregational histories on the Internet.

I would particularly like to recognize the important contributions of my partner on this project, Cynthia Prescott. She first suggested the history of the fellowship movement to me as a topic for a term paper on Unitarian Universalist history in 2001, my first year in seminary. She collaborated with me on writing a proposal for funding from the Fund for Unitarian Universalism, which enabled us to visit many of these fellowship congregations. Cynthia helped me assemble an advisory board, worked with me in the initial focus groups, went with me on four different trips to visit congregations and district executives, and helped me process those experiences afterwards. A book such as this could only have come about through a clergy-lay collaboration, because the story needed both perspectives. Shared ministry is one of the major gifts of the lay-led fellowship movement, one that has certainly been very much alive in the creation of this historical account.

A Growth Strategy for a New Era

In 1948 the economy was in the midst of a postwar economic boom. Part of that era was the baby boom, which lasted for eighteen years (1946–1964), and spawned a demand for religious education for children and religious communities for highly mobile nuclear families. Those fellowships that grew and thrived almost always developed strong religious education programs for this generation at a very early stage in the congregation's development.

The U.S. population was relocating, away from the Northeast, toward the South and West and parts of the Midwest. Migrants took their religious habits with them, and often that religious habit was Unitarian, creating for some fellowships a nucleus of people who knew what Unitarianism was and bringing that knowledge into new settings.

From long before the 1961 merger, Unitarians have shared with Universalists a commitment to creating heaven on earth, preaching and practicing the social gospel. The two great nineteenth-century social movements in which both Unitarians and Universalists were deeply engaged, abolition of slavery and women's suffrage, saw the rise of "descendent" social movements in the 1950s and 1960s in the civil rights and feminist movements. Toward the end of the fellowship era (1948–1967), the antiwar and environmental movements began to gather steam as well, broadening the range of opportunities for social activism. For many who might otherwise have remained unchurched, lay-led fellowships often provided an environment in which these three activist social change movements could be grounded in religious community.

The GI Bill sent many ex-soldiers to college in the 1950s. They were followed by the children of the baby boomers, so the 1950s and 1960s saw a great expansion in the college population and with that, a growth of college faculty and college communities. Unitarianism has always had a strongly intellectual component. Under the sway of the humanist movement of the 1920s and 1930s, Sunday services in even traditional Unitarian churches had shifted their emphasis toward the intellectual and away from some of the more emotional, spiritual, and ritualistic elements of worship, a trend particularly appealing to many academics. Almost always more liberal, politically and religiously, than the surrounding society, these growing college communities were especially fertile ground for planting the Unitarian religious flag in new regions of the country.

The fellowship movement, then, was born and grew to maturity during times that were ripe for such a religious movement. It appealed to people moving from region to region who were looking for a religious community in which to put down roots and raise their large brood of baby boomers and engage with the pressing social issues of the day. At the same time, these fellowships provided religious homes for a growing academic community and an expanding population of educated professionals.

Origins

Lay-led groups were not a new concept for Unitarianism, or Universalism, or to Protestant Christianity in general. In Europe during and after the Reformation, "house churches" were common among the nonestablished churches, including Methodists, Quakers, and Anabaptists—Christian denominations that were tolerated but not financially supported by the government. As the name suggests, members of house churches met informally in their homes and usually did not have a minister.

Quakers still do not have professional clergy, nor do some other denominations, such as Jehovah's Witnesses. But the Unitarian fellowship movement created lay-led congregations that coexisted within the same denomination with congregations served by clergy. This model was more unusual, although not unique.

Laile Bartlett and Rev. Dan O'Neal, both of whom studied the fellowship movement, traced its origins as far back as English Unitarian leader Joseph Priestley, who had recommended the organization of such lay societies in 1793. The fellowship movement also has roots in ideas about lay circles or Sunday circles in the 1880s and 1890s. Among the Universalists, Quillen Shinn traveled throughout the Southeast in the late 19th century creating many small, rural, lay-led congregations that could be considered forerunners of lay-led fellowships in the mid-20th century.

In 1907, a proposal adopted by the American Unitarian Association called for the creation of lay-led societies, but the concept was very different from the one ultimately adopted in 1948. These societies were to be managed in a very top-down, "church-in-a-box" fashion, providing complete worship services and religious education programs and a standardized structure, with little room for local initiative. The goal was to grow them to church size, at which point they would follow the normal pattern of acquiring a building and calling a minister. This strategy met with almost no success.

The radical change undertaken in 1948 was to give far greater autonomy to local groups. In doing so, the New England-based AUA continued the practice of its forebears, the Congregationalists, who strongly affirmed congregational polity, in which local congregations govern themselves. Under this system, the larger association credentials ministers, establishes the boundaries of faith and doctrine, and provides support of various kinds. But the final authority to manage property, finances, and other affairs, including calling and dismissing ministers, rests with the congregation. The concept of congregational polity flowed naturally into the new Unitarian denomination when it was created in 1825, as many former Congregational churches became Unitarian. In adopting congregational polity, however, neither the Congregationalists nor the Unitarians envisioned the further step of not having any minister present in a congregation. This expansion of the concept of congregational polity was the central innovation in establishing lay-led fellowships.

The Beginnings of a Movement

The fellowship movement owes its inception to three people. One was Frederick May Eliot, president of the AUA in the 1940s. The second was Rev. Lon Ray Call, AUA minister-at-large, who was available "on loan" to congregations in need of short-term guidance and encouragement. The third was Munroe Husbands, the first and only director of the fellowship program. Each of these three men played a key role in recognizing the potential of lay-led fellowships to meet specific challenges of the times

As president, Eliot was concerned about the AUA's declining membership and precarious financial situation. The humanist movement of the 1920s and 1930s had created deep divisions between theists and humanists, adding to existing divisions between Christian and non-Christian theists. After World War II, the AUA found itself hampered by lack of money, declining membership, and a shortage of clergy. It was also stuck in a catch-22—to attract more members, it needed more churches; but to get the money to start those churches, it needed more members.

The AUA's existing model for starting new congregations included full-time clerical leadership from the beginning and a long period of financial subsidy. According to O'Neal,

> Denominational officials...would scout out likely areas to start new churches. These areas had to meet certain criteria, such as population requirements. Headquarters would generally only subsidize three groups a year. And the truth of the matter was that there were no ministers available for

> such duties anyway. . . . The usual work of extension had to be curtailed. How could an aggressive extension program be conducted under these limiting conditions?

The few new starts that could be managed under that model were limited to urban areas, where a congregation could be expected to grow to self-sufficiency fairly rapidly. There was no money to waste on small groups with limited growth potential. New congregations needed to be an investment, not a liability.

It made sense for the AUA to concentrate its limited resources in urban areas with the greatest potential. However, as Lon Ray Call pointed out to the board of the AUA, opportunities were being overlooked in many smaller communities that had potential to develop at least medium-sized Unitarian congregations. In these communities, a lack of funds rather than a lack of interest prevented the Unitarian flag from being planted.

Not having a congregation frustrated isolated or small clusters of Unitarians, who could find no acceptable religious alternative. A Presbyterian who found herself in a community without a church of her own denomination might fit comfortably into a Methodist congregation, or a Lutheran might transition into an Episcopal community; but the distance between Unitarians and traditional trinitarian Christianity was usually too wide a gap to bridge.

The situation was equally frustrating for the AUA. With the U.S. population increasing rapidly and shifting away from Unitarianism's traditional home in the Northeast, the Extension Department saw enormous growth potential that it could not tap. The AUA needed a new strategy, a creative response to the challenge of limited resources.

Part of the inspiration for the new fellowship movement came from the Church of the Larger Fellowship (CLF). The CLF was founded in 1944 to serve isolated religious liberals by sending them materials through the mail. Some of the CLF's members assembled in clusters—too small for a church, but large enough for some sort of connection with each other. Wherever two or three liberal religious individuals or households were gathered together, there was a possibility of creating some sort of religious community for them. A lay-led fellowship seemed to the AUA leadership like a feasible form of extension for smaller communities.

At the same time, lay-led fellowships might provide a solution to another problem: how to help congregations in decline. These congregations, many of them in New England, could no longer support a full-fledged program and professional ministry. Yet they still wanted to retain their identity as Unitarians and some connection to a liberal religious community. AUA President Frederick May Eliot reported that the question of how to deal with declining congregations had been posed to him this way: "Is there some form of church organization less costly and demanding than the ordinary parish with a minister, but also a more cohesive group than can be achieved by the Church of the Larger Fellowship?"

Lon Ray Call investigated the numerous failures and closures of Unitarian churches that had occurred since 1900. He came to a similar conclusion about the potential for lay-led fellowships to provide a scaled-down church experience for the members of struggling congregations. As it turned out, however, the fellowship program was used almost exclusively for starting new groups rather than sustaining declining ones.

In 1945, the AUA board created a committee to study the issue. Call served on this committee, bringing to it his extensive experience with small or emerging congregations around the country. He argued that the 1907 experiment in creating lay societies failed because it was too rigid, too top-down. Any new attempt to form lay-led societies should be much more flexible and less hierarchical. That recommendation shaped the plan proposed to the AUA board by the study committee in 1947, when they requested and received funds for an office and a director.

Munroe Husbands defined fellowships this way in 1949:

> Ten or more religious liberals living in an community where there is no Unitarian church (or a suburb of a large city that

> does support a church) may become a Unitarian fellowship when they have expressed their approval or sympathy with the purposes of the Association and when their contributions are received and have been accepted by the Board of Directors. Fellowships are eligible to send one voting delegate to all meetings of the Association and will be listed in the annual Year Book.

The newly created Fellowship Office in Boston that served those small groups was part of the Department of Extension and Church Maintenance, often referred to as the Extension Department. The responsibility for planting and nurturing lay-led groups fell primarily on one man, Husbands. A layperson, he served as both director of the fellowship program and clerk of the Church of the Larger Fellowship, forging a link between the two programs. For the first ten years, he ran the Fellowship Office with just one assistant. When the program was formally launched in May 1948, Husbands began almost 20 years of crisscrossing the country, meeting with small groups and leaving seedling fellowships in his wake.

The Mission and Purpose of Fellowship

There was no single vision for this experiment in church growth. Some AUA leaders saw fellowships as a way to provide liberal religious communities for smaller towns that did not have the critical mass to support a full-service church. Others thought that the most important aspect of fellowships was developing leadership and spiritual qualities among the laity through sermon preparation and other efforts at religious leadership. In this view, a fellowship's success was measured not by it "growing up to be a church," but by its ability to serve its members' religious needs. A fellowship, with a little guidance, could address the needs for affiliation, self-actualization, and religious community. For some people, small size and the opportunities for lay leadership were essential to meet those needs.

It was clear from the outset that the fellowship movement would create groups larger than the isolated individuals and families served by the Church of the Larger Fellowship. But not all of them would be expected or pressured to grow into churches, although growth was encouraged. Lon Ray Call insisted that a fellowship was not a church ". . . and should not be thought of being the first step toward a church except in very promising cities." Nevertheless, in Boston there was still a hope that many fellowships would develop into churches—large churches, churches that would be assets and would generate funding to continue the work and expansion of the faith movement.

In some places that hope was realized. Many fellowships eventually built or purchased buildings and either called ordained clergy or ordained their own lay ministers. But some fellowships stayed small and lay-led. Others grew and called ministers, but chewed them up and spit them out because laypersons, once empowered with religious authority, were unwilling to give it up or even to share. As reports of conflict and chaos multiplied, there was growing concern in Boston that the fellowship program had unleashed a monster.

The Extension Department recognized that the movement, whatever its goals, also had positive effects. In a 1949 memo, Munroe Husbands pointed out that these fellowships were meeting the needs of individuals, of nearby churches, and of the AUA. For individuals, there was the pleasure and satisfaction of religious affiliation. For nearby churches, fellowships could be a companion rather than a drain, a means of greater visibility leading to growth in both churches and fellowships. Often fellowships developed fraternal relations with nearby churches, sometimes visiting for worship, inviting the minister to fill their pulpit, or collaborating with them in other ways. For the AUA, the investment needed to transition an already established, viable fellowship into a church with minister and building was far less than the cost of starting a new congregation from scratch.

Ultimately, the fellowship movement had benefits that few

would have predicted. In a 2004 sermon, Rev. Lisa Schwartz described the somewhat unexpected outcome this way:

> From a denominational perspective, it's safe to assume that the intended purpose of starting small, lay-led Unitarian fellowships was that they would grow and mature into "real" churches. Remember that a "culture of sameness" held sway, a culture that assumed that there was only one way to do church, because of course everybody coming to church needed pretty much the same thing. Well, a strange and really wonderful thing happened: many of these lay-led Unitarian fellowships began to experiment with new ways to do church—partly out of necessity, since they had no minister or staff, and partly because the fellowship movement tended to attract innovative thinkers, people who didn't easily accept the status quo and who chafed under creedal requirements. Free from the restrictive bonds that might have kept the neighborhood of Boston in line, small groups in the Midwest and beyond could throw out all the assumptions about The Right Way to do Sunday school, or worship, and start writing a new chapter on a fresh page. Many of the people who started and grew Unitarian fellowships in the 40s and 50s were pioneers, blazing a trail out of the culture of sameness, away from the assumption that the bland Protestant soup of the day would satisfy all spiritual hunger.

The fellowship movement as a deliberate strategy of growth and expansion lasted not quite 20 years, but it has left a permanent mark on Unitarian Universalism. The story officially began in Boulder, Colorado, in July 1948, when the first fellowship was chartered. Stillwater, Oklahoma, had hoped to be first, but was a tad too slow in processing its paperwork and instead came in second. They were followed in quick succession by Beaumont, Texas; San Gabriel Valley, California; and Ames, Iowa. Significantly, three of these five communities were home to large state universities. By January 1949, Husbands reported 13 fully organized fellowships, including four on the West Coast—two in California and two in Washington—and only one in the Northeast (Northport, New York). This start in college towns and in the West was a portent of things to come.

Many Seedlings Make a Forest

Most congregations that were born as fellowships between 1948 and 1967, in telling their creation stories, describe a similar pattern of events. A pastiche of typical stories about the formation of fellowships would sound something like this: "Two or three of us met over coffee and decided to contact Boston. . . . We placed an ad in the newspaper and lined up a meeting space. . . . Munroe Husbands came from Boston and met with us. . . . At the end of the evening we had signed up more members than we expected and were on our way." Some fellowships managed to come into existence without such a visit, relying on literature and distant advice from Boston.

A fellowship's first public meeting involved extensive advance work in developing a list of potential participants, finding a public room, and placing newspaper ads. Much of the newspaper advertising was sponsored by an AUA men's organization called the Laymen's League. This group also placed ads in magazines frequently read by religious and political liberals, providing additional local contacts to the Fellowship Office. One ad read:

> What's your idea of true religion?
> Unitarianism is a way of life, life of vigorous thought, constructive activity, of generous service—not a religion of inherited creeds, revered saints, or holy books.

> Unitarianism is not an easy religion. It demands that people think out their beliefs for themselves, and then live those beliefs. The stress is placed upon living this life nobly and effectively rather than on the preparation for an after-existence.
>
> If you have given up "old time" religion, Unitarianism has the answer for you.

Another advertisement read:

> This is the Unitarian Idea
> Unitarian churches are dedicated to the progressive transformation and ennoblement of individual and social life, through religion, in accordance with the advancing knowledge and the growing vision of mankind.
>
> In Religion
> Freedom is our Method
> Reason is our Guide
> Fellowship is our Spirit
> Character is our Test
> Service is our Goal

If enough responses to an ad were received in an area, a visit from Munroe Husbands was arranged. At the public meeting, Husbands would give a basic talk about Unitarianism. This would be followed by questions, discussion, and the passing of an attendance sheet. If there was enough interest, a steering committee would be formed. This group would be provided with an organizational guide, a fellowship manual, a leadership guide, and a handbook for planning programs. If the need was indicated, materials on religious education would also be provided.

If a group took shape, the next step was to write bylaws and a statement of purpose, which would be filed with the Fellowship Office. Together with a list of at least ten people who had signed the membership roll and made a financial contribution, this act qualified the group as a fellowship, a voting member of the American Unitarian Association.

Having attained recognition from the AUA, the group looked for a place to hold regular meetings. They then embarked on a series of discussions on "Controversial Religious Problems," based on materials from the AUA's Fellowship Office that were prepared by Lon Ray Call. The controversial issues were:

Jesus: God, Man, or Myth?
God: Person, Force, or Phantom?
Are Unitarians Christian?
Prayer—To Whom and for What?
Is Death the End?
What Are We Here For?

Any seminary graduate would recognize these topics as central elements of building a liberal systematic theology not grounded solely in the Christian scriptures. Even today, a popular adult curriculum, *Building Your Own Theology* by Rev. Richard Gilbert, encourages participants to explore many of these same questions. For fledgling fellowships, full of newcomers to Unitarianism, addressing these fundamental theological issues was an essential step in self-definition.

Spin-offs and Splinters

Some fellowships tell a somewhat different creation story. New congregations could also arise out of an existing congregation as either a friendly spin-off or a rebellious splinter group. Many spin-offs and almost all splinter groups began as lay-led fellowships.

A spin-off starts with the support of a nearby established congregation, which nurtures it until it is ready to function on its own. The most dramatic example is a cluster of congregations that spun off from All Souls Church, a Unitarian congregation in Washington, D.C. All Souls was under the leadership of A. Powell Davies in the 1940s and 1950s. He refused to let Munroe Husbands organize lay-led fellowships in the area around the nation's capital. Davies instead arranged for small groups to congregate in various suburban areas and listen to the service "piped in" from All Souls. Many of these groups, with continuing support and assistance from All Souls, grew into churches and called ministers, including Alexandria and Arlington in Virginia and Bethesda and Camp Springs in Maryland. The Camp Springs congregation bears the name Davies Memorial Church in honor of Davies's contribution to their existence.

Spin-offs took place in many regions of the country. Buffalo, New York, was the parent of the Hamberg fellowship, while Asheville, North Carolina, was responsible for fostering several new congregations during and after the period of the fellowship movement. Congregations in the Dallas and Denver areas report providing similar aid in the early years, as do congregations on the West Coast, from Southern California to British Columbia. The Vancouver Unitarian Church spun off several new congregations, including North Shore, Beacon, and South Fraser. The Tulsa congregation nurtured a number of fledgling fellowships in Oklahoma, including one in Stillwater. Sometimes, as in the case of Stillwater, it is difficult to make a clear distinction between spin-offs and fellowships that arose independently but received support from a nearby congregation.

Like spin-offs, splinter groups arose from existing congregations. But rather than being nurtured by the parent congregation, they broke away on their own. In a few cases, the splinter group took the majority; more often, it was a smaller group that broke away. Sometimes the break was a result of conflict. Other times, the splinter group arose out of nothing more than a desire for the small, intimate, informal atmosphere of a lay-led fellowship.

Munroe Husbands's Travels

The archives of the UUA contain countless reports of Munroe Husbands's exhausting trips to start new congregations, beginning in 1949. His annual reports were generally upbeat and detailed. The April 1954 annual report, for example, identified 135 affiliated fellowships, including 29 organized that year. Four fellowships had folded that year, and two had become churches with the assistance of the AUA and a minister-at-large. Husbands's report also included a long list of services to fellowships, a loan program for fellowships that were building or acquiring property, and a summer student minister program.

As usual, Husbands reported on two field trips that year. His spring trip was a southern swing that lasted 37 days, covered about 7,500 miles, and involved 38 communities. He visited four churches and 13 existing fellowships, met with 13 potential fellowships, and made exploratory stops to "case" two communities (Danville, Virginia, and Salisbury, Maryland) as potential fellowship sites. His first stop was State College, Pennsylvania, an established fellowship. The trip took him as far as Texas (Austin, Temple, Waco, Abilene, San Angelo, Midland, Lubbock, and Amarillo) and Oklahoma (Norman, Ada, Stillwater, Bartlesville, and Tulsa), with other stops in Kansas, Missouri, Louisiana, Mississippi, Alabama, Tennessee, West Virginia, Virginia, and North Carolina.

The stories of some stops on Husbands's tour were encouraging. Nashville was ready to become a church. Congregations in State College, Austin, Amarillo, Asheville, Shreveport, Baton Rouge, Roanoke, and Bartlesville appeared to be thriving. Formational meetings in Manhattan and Parsons, Kansas; Morgantown, West Virginia; Springfield, Missouri; and Tyler, Temple, and Midland, Texas, all seemed to be going well. Smaller congregations in Biloxi, Mississippi, and Mobile, Alabama, seemed promising.

Other stops were less successful. There seemed to be few interested prospects in Florence, Alabama; Lafayette, Louisiana; Waco, San Angelo, and Abilene, Texas; Ada, Oklahoma; and Hattiesburg, Mississippi. Husbands also found congregations in some disarray, including Norman and Stillwater, Oklahoma, and Chattanooga, Tennessee.

His fall trip that year was another 37-day marathon with 37 stops. This time Husbands traveled to the north central part of the country—chiefly Michigan, Wisconsin, Minnesota, and North

Dakota, with several stops in Canada (Ontario, Saskatchewan, and Manitoba). He even encountered a hurricane on the way. Again, Husbands found some of his earlier plantings bearing fruit in St. Catharines, Ontario; Midland, Michigan; and Bismarck, North Dakota. Others were floundering. Meetings to organize a congregation looked promising in Battle Creek and Saginaw, Michigan, and in Hibbing and St. Cloud, Minnesota. Other exploratory meetings did not turn up a critical mass of prospective members. Husbands complained of poor advance work at several visits. He found himself consulting with some previously planted fellowships to keep them going and get them over the rough spots.

Many of the congregations that Husbands visited on these trips are still in existence some 50 years later. The Johnny Appleseed of Unitarianism, unlike his legendary tree-planting counterpart, did not just plant. He also stopped back to water, fertilize, and visit with his plantings on his travels through the country.

Birthing Pains

Newly organized fellowships ran into several immediate challenges. One was finding a suitable meeting space. Many groups started out meeting in a member's living room, but found they needed to graduate fairly quickly to a larger, more public, more visible location. (The March 1959 issue of the *Unitarian Fellowship Newsletter* noted that 11 of 30 fellowships that had died were among those that met exclusively in members' homes rather than in public places.) Rental space was often hard to find and not well suited to the purpose. A fellowship needed not just a large gathering space, but also a kitchen for hospitality, one or more smaller rooms for religious education, and a place to store the group's possessions, which might include a banner, hymnals, religious education materials, and other paraphernalia. Fellowships turned to a variety of rented meeting spaces: houses, radio stations, municipal and school auditoriums, YMCAs, synagogues, storefronts, hotels. A fellowship in Davis, California, rented a

Girl Scout cabin. Eventually, most fellowships that flourished addressed the need to obtain a building of their own, as described in "Becoming Churches."

From the beginning, fellowships also struggled with the content of the Sunday morning gathering. In a note to Lon Ray Call in September 1947, Unitarian minister Bill Lovely of Austin expressed concern about this issue. He said,

> The heart of your problem will be the selection and training of lay leaders. People need *religious* services. They need a group to which they can turn for fellowship in religious living, and such sacraments as funeral[s] and christening[s], etc. For these things they turn now to Methodists, Episcopalians, etc., etc. Liberals need a liberal church—but as religious, normal people, *they need a church*, liberal or not. Therefore, your lay leaders must be willing and able to lead in worship and special services. Discussion, education, action can be led by enthusiasts on the basis of secular education and experience—but "religious" services take a lot of specialized information and training. The fact that liberals are so diverse in their attitudes toward "sacraments," "prayers," "aspirations," "scripture," "God," "Jesus," etc. makes the job of serving them in a religious way more difficult.
>
> It is, then, to summarize, pointless to set up a religious group which cannot offer religious services. The quality of those religious services will depend on 1) the material which can be put in the hands of your lay leader, and 2) the skill with which he can adapt it to local and individual needs.

Lovely's advice to provide training in worship was largely ignored by the Fellowship Office. From 1948 until the present day, controversy over the form and content of the Sunday morning event has dogged lay-led fellowships, as well as the first ministers of formerly lay-led congregations. The chapter on "Fellowship Culture" will return to that story.

Another challenge faced by newly formed fellowships was the demand for children's religious education. The original vision for lay-led fellowships did not give much thought to involving children. Materials were designed with adult discussion groups in mind. But the baby boom of the 1940s and 1950s created a huge market for programs for children and youth. Thus, many fellowships started church schools early in their development.

In her history of the fellowship movement, *Bright Galaxy,* Laile Bartlett describes one initial meeting to explore starting a fellowship: While the parents tried to create a religious home for themselves and their families, 75 children were outside playing in the yard. The Princeton, New Jersey, fellowship held its first worship service on Easter Sunday in 1948 with 47 adults and 48 children in attendance. The Carbondale, Illinois, fellowship, formed in a college town in 1952, emphasized religious education from the start. According to the congregation's historian, Lillian Adams, most of the founders of the Carbondale fellowship were parents who wanted nontraditional religious education for their children. A focus on religious education was the magnet that enabled this congregation to grow into a building in 1956 and to appoint an extension minister in 1997.

Many fellowships labeled their religious education programs "junior fellowships." A few fellowships, including both the Marin County and Mount Diablo congregations in California, were actually born for the purpose of creating a church school, with an adult program growing up around it. For many parents, the opportunity to provide their children with eclectic, nondogmatic religious education was the primary reason for belonging to a fellowship. Parents came because of the children, even though many remained long after the children had grown up.

This predictable, but often unanticipated, influx of children created several challenges for fellowships. One issue was finding an appropriate facility. Adults can meet pretty much anywhere, but children need specialized space and equipment. Religious education programs put pressure on fellowships to find relatively permanent quarters.

In addition, it takes more training and materials to teach children than to run adult discussion groups. The do-it-yourself mentality of many lay-led fellowships was put to the test by the need for religious education. Some fellowships were forced to call on the regional conference or the national association for help.

The AUA Fellowship Office responded by adding a *Religious Education Manual for Fellowships* to its set of basic materials on fellowship organization, planning, leadership, and management. The manual noted that "no fellowship will grow and continue in strength unless it sponsors a church school." The small AUA Division of Education sent its two field workers to fellowships, offering advice, literature, and technical assistance. Lay-led fellowships also benefited from the innovative and engaging curricula for children and youth developed by Sophia Lyon Fahs and other pioneers in liberal religious education in the 1930s and 1940s. To meet the challenge of developing a quality children's religious education program, the first professional staff hired by many fellowships was not a minister, but a director of religious education, usually part time.

The third challenge related to accommodating children—one faced by not only emerging fellowships, but small congregations in general—was the size of the group. A critical mass of children is needed in order to offer a graded curriculum. Fellowships might have a dozen or so children and youth ranging in age from 3 to 17. The age differential is too large to create a single class, but dividing into appropriate age groups creates very small classes. The absence of just one family on a given Sunday can leave a class of one or two students. Teachers must adjust curricula and plan more activities that work for a greater age span. The one-room schoolhouse, largely banished from public education, reemerged in many lay-led congregations. Ultimately, the desire for a quality religious education program was often the deciding factor that pushed fellowships out of their family-style comfort zone and into accepting the need for growth.

Stages of Growth

Munroe Husbands saw fellowships passing through a series of developmental stages and plateaus. In the first stage, the fellowship is small and intimate. Enthusiasm and a sense of discovery or invention are high, and the administrative work is fairly easy. Everyone pitches in. This might be described as the honeymoon stage. Husbands called it the "organizational phase."

After about a year, the fellowship reaches a plateau in terms of membership. Husbands labeled this stage "first-year disillusionment." The nonproselytizing approach of Unitarians created the expectation that new members would find the fellowship on their own. Once the initial group had joined, membership sometimes remained static for months or even years. As a further barrier to growth, members were likely to be highly satisfied with the size of the group, finding it comfortable for discussions, social activities, and getting to know everyone well. The plateau of the first year was followed by a second and sometimes third year in which the group realized that they needed more active engagement to grow the fellowship.

The next step varied greatly from one fellowship to another, but generally came when membership grew to about 40 to 50 families. At this point, the fellowship started thinking seriously about either a building or staff. A common sequence was to begin staffing the fellowship with a part-time secretary or office administrator, then a director of religious education.

According to Husbands, the last plateau was reached when the fellowship had too many jobs and too few leaders. The congregation had to either call a minister and commit to continued growth, or split into smaller, more manageable groups. Some fellowships never arrived at the last plateau. Most of those that did eventually became churches—not necessarily in name, but in terms of worship, religious education, a building, and professional ministry.

While many fellowships reached one plateau and stayed there, some fellowships folded. Bartlett identified 28 fellowships that ceased to exist in the first decade, primarily because of leadership problems. Of those, 26 had not established a children's religious education program, and 11 met only in homes. The average life of these failed starts was just over two and a half years.

The First Ten Years

Fellowships were not the only way to start new congregations during this time. The AUA continued to plant a limited number of new clergy-led congregations in larger communities, such as New Haven, Connecticut; Charlotte, North Carolina; and San Antonio, Texas. But the lay-led fellowship was the principal vehicle for creating new Unitarian congregations.

In the first ten years of the fellowship movement, from 1948 to 1958, a total of 323 lay-led Unitarian fellowships were organized. These fellowships attracted 12,500 members, one-third of total membership growth in that decade. Three-fourths of these fellowship members were new to Unitarianism. These achievements are even more remarkable considering that all of the travel to sustain developing fellowships and plant new ones fell largely to Munroe Husbands.

The most fertile grounds for developing lay-led fellowships in the first ten years were far from Boston—they were found on the West Coast, the South, the Southwest and the Midwest. California, Oregon, and Washington alone spawned nearly one-fifth of the 275 fellowships established by 1958. Munroe Husbands's 1956 expedition to the territory of Alaska resulted in four surviving fellowships, while another 15 fellowships were established in Canada.

In a 1956 internal memo in the Extension Department, director Richard Gibbs expressed some concerns about the fellowship movement and its service demands. He wrote,

> We now have a lay movement of approximately 5,000 unsupervised directly by the denomination. It is a serious question whether one man and his secretary can continue to serve this effectively and perhaps more important, begin to handle what can be 10,000 of these people in fellowships in the near future.

In 1956 the AUA appointed two ministers-at-large to serve the fellowship program. The ministers-at-large worked with fellowships that had reached the level of 40 to 50 families, helping them grow to a size that could support full-time ministry. Regional directors were asked to identify fellowships that were candidates for this service, based on size, community potential, the will to grow, experienced leadership, and other criteria.

Even with that additional staffing, by 1958 the attention of the Fellowship Office was becoming increasingly divided between the demands of new starts and the support of the fledgling fellowships, 29 of which had already "graduated" to church status. Munroe Husbands replaced his one assistant with two secretaries to handle the increased workload. The second phase of the fellowship movement was about to begin.

The End of an Experiment

From 1958 to 1967, the work of the Fellowship Office was carried out primarily by director Munroe Husbands and minister-at-large Grant Butler, who had replaced Lon Ray Call in that role. Their efforts resulted in the founding of an additional 135 congregations that still survive. But throughout this period, the number of new starts per year steadily decreased, ultimately leading to the end of the official fellowship program.

In his annual report for fiscal year 1958–59, Husbands wrote that 55 new fellowships had been organized, 13 had transitioned from fellowship to church, and 5 had disbanded. The 55 congregations proved to be a high water mark for new starts in a single year. The calendar year 1958 also holds the record for the creation of surviving first-wave fellowships—33.

From that peak, a slowdown began. Between 1961 and 1965, the Extension Department of the newly formed Unitarian Universalist Association recorded 164 new fellowships organized, as well as 4 mergers, 19 fellowships that became churches, and 55 that folded. The last recorded field trip by Todd Taylor, Husbands's assistant, was in the spring of 1967. In this 11-day trip to Ohio, Indiana, Illinois, Missouri, Iowa, and Minnesota, Taylor made ten stops. Only four of the stops were to organize new fellowships; the others were visits to existing congregations. In the final six months of the Fellowship Office in 1967, only seven new fellowships were organized.

This slowdown can be attributed in part to the flagging energy and limited budget of the small staff. In 1957, for example, the Universalists asked the American Unitarian Association to match their contribution of $2,500 to start a joint fellowship in an Ohio community. The offer was declined, in part because the AUA was not yet ready to join forces at that level. However, the primary reason was money. Husbands noted that his entire budget for that year was only $2,300, with which he was expected to start 25 new fellowships and service the existing ones.

But there were also other reasons for the steady decline in new fellowships. Just as congregations reach growth plateaus, so did the movement as a whole. The program had already planted fellowships in the most promising communities, leaving fewer targets for additional growth. In addition, the fellowships that had been established in earlier years needed care and feeding from the Fellowship Office, limiting the resources available for new starts.

An internal memo from extension director Richard Gibbs acknowledged that the fellowship movement had been a percentage game:

> We have said organize as many as we can as fast as we can, knowing that between 7 and 10 percent will fold up in a given year. We have said they have to sink or swim because so far we have been unable to give them much personal attention either on the headquarters or district level. Some have argued it would be better to organize fewer and give them the attention they need to develop their full potential. Maybe so, at any rate so far we have chosen the other route.

In his April 1959 report, Munroe Husbands noted a shift in the goals and expectations of the fellowship program. Originally, he observed, growth was the primary concern. But by 1958–59, it was service, since

> requests for financial assistance, religious educational guidance, aids with adult programming and help with special problems come from fellowships. The regions, sub-regions and headquarters are doing their best to meet these requests; personnel and financial limitations have been a handicap. But this is our challenge.

He also noted, peripherally, that failing fellowships generally started out with the bare minimum of ten members, and that perhaps the minimum size should be raised to 15. But his main concern was addressing the service needs of the large number of lay-led fellowships that had started under his nurture and guidance.

In the midst of the fellowship movement, the Unitarians and Universalists merged in 1961, when the Universalist Church of America, dwindling in numbers, reluctantly agreed to join with the American Unitarian Association. The Universalists had embraced the fellowship model in the late 1950s, calling their lay-led congregations "circles," although they only established a handful of congregations before the merger.

The years following the merger saw a loss of denominational support for the fellowship approach to extension. In part, this lack of support reflected the frustration of ministers who unsuccessfully tried to serve formerly lay-led fellowships—as will be described in the chapters "Fellowship Culture" and "Becoming Churches." Another factor was the precarious financial condition of the UUA in the late 1960s.

The end of the fellowship movement came with the loss of two key staff members—the death of minister-at-large Grant Butler in 1967 and the retirement of Munroe Husbands in the same year. With the UUA in difficult financial circumstances, neither of them was replaced. The loss of staff leadership effectively put the fellowship movement on hold. This suspension was initially designated as temporary, but ultimately became permanent. The post-merger UUA took a different approach to growth.

In an Extension Department memo dated July 20, 1967, Robert S. Wolley listed the highest priorities of the department: the Church of the Larger Fellowship, the minister-at-large program, metropolitan extension (new urban churches), and routine correspondence. He then stated,

> The items of varying importance which will have to be dropped for a time include fellowship organizing, the fellowship program exchange and Newsletter, weekend workshops, surveys and special projects, and generalized "trouble-shooting" field visits. The district liaison function carried on by the former director [Husbands] has been transferred to the Executive Vice President.

In other words, the field work that had been the primary function of the Fellowship Office was ended. The activities of the Fellowship Office were subsumed into the Extension Department. The work of starting up new lay-led fellowships and nurturing them through the early years was largely dispersed to the districts, where it remains to this day, although the UUA provides active support for this work through the Congregational Services department.

Recognition Comes to Munroe Husbands

The pivotal role of Munroe Husbands did not go unacknowledged. In 1974, the UUA gave Husbands its Annual Award for Distinguished Service to the Cause of Liberal Religion. The citation by Christopher Raible reads:

> To Munroe Husbands—circuit rider of mid-20th century, organizer of more Unitarian Universalist congregations than any one person in our history, personification of liberal religious extension.
>
> For nearly two decades you gave of yourself to strengthen our corporate existence through encouraging, nurturing, cherishing fellowships of free persons. Before you came to

the American Unitarian Association in 1948, the program was so strange that it had not staff nor budget nor even name. Not everyone applauded, but you insisted and then proved that the fellowship program could succeed. You showed that religious societies can be created without benefit of clergy and still be legitimate.

Your long, often lonely labors wore out automobiles, wore down doubters, very nearly wore out your own health. Your travels and your constant personal attention shortened the distance between us as congregations and as persons. Your words—spoken, telephoned, written, printed—carried your contagious confidence in the vitality of liberal religion, and in its need to be organized. As a layman, your words and your life spoke to laymen—and to us all.

Veatch to the Rescue

An important part of the rationale for deciding to close the Fellowship Office was the precarious financial condition of the UUA in the late 1960s. Warren Ross, in *Funding Justice: The Legacy of the Unitarian Universalist Veatch Program*, reports that when President Robert West took office in 1969 he found that the association was deep in debt and running a $1 million budget deficit. The UUA eventually emerged from its financial difficulties with help from an unlikely source. In 1953 the Shelter Rock congregation on Long Island had received a generous bequest in the will of one of its members, Caroline Veatch. Over the years, the royalty income from the bequest mounted and the congregation eventually established the Veatch Foundation, to fund social justice initiatives and to assist the denomination. In 1969, the foundation began to help bail the UUA out of its crisis.

Some of the Veatch Foundation's programs were of particular value to first-wave fellowships. For example, the foundation established a fund to help Unitarian Universalist congregations construct church buildings. Many fellowships also benefited from the extension ministry program (discussed in "Becoming Churches").

The closing of the Fellowship Office did not preclude the development of new lay-led fellowships, just the withdrawal of encouragement, support, and assistance. Part of the rationale was financial, but there was also growing concern about the kinds of congregations that had arisen, which were very different from the established Unitarian and Unitarian Universalist congregations of an earlier era. The special characteristics of these new congregations were often characterized by the term "fellowship culture," to which we now turn our attention.

Fellowship Culture

The distinction between a fellowship and a church goes beyond structural definitions such as the size of the group or how it was formed. Lay-led fellowships—and to some extent, formerly lay-led fellowships that have since called a minister—share certain characteristics that set them apart from other congregations.

No one is quite sure of the origins of the phrase "fellowship culture," but it is clear that most people do not use the term positively. On the plus side, fellowships tend to be lively, empowering, innovative, and close-knit. But they can also be chaotic, resistant to authority and structure, and opposed to growth. One thing is certain: To understand the fellowship movement—and the past, present, and future of the congregations it gave birth to—one must understand fellowship culture.

Laile Bartlett, who wrote the early history of the fellowship movement, saw the essence of fellowship culture as not just limited size, but "an atmosphere of permissiveness and freedom." She was one of the few enthusiastic supporters of fellowship culture. In *Bright Galaxy*, she offers this description:

> It is a youthful spirit, with most of the qualities one associates with youth. It is eager, fresh, vigorous, energetic, hard-

> working, and alive. It is brusque, awkward, spontaneous, tripping over its own slightly-too-large feet. It is often inconsiderate, sometimes gauche. There are stars in its eyes and dreams in its heart. It is eager to learn and boundlessly ambitious. It can do anything. . . . There is curiosity—questioning and seeking, questioning and seeking, endlessly. There are dependence on its elders and great expectations from them—but a wild rejection of them, too, in the self-assertive, independent awareness that "I can do it all myself."

For Bartlett, fellowship culture was to be celebrated. In her view, fellowship culture empowered the laity, encouraged experimentation, and introduced a new vitality into a stagnant faith tradition.

Certainly lay empowerment and openness to experimentation remain vital elements of fellowship culture in many congregations today. But so do some of the less attractive aspects of fellowship culture. Even Bartlett admitted that fellowships too often emphasize freedom *from* rather than freedom *to*—defining themselves by what they are not or what they are against. For some first-wave fellowships, that negative self-definition was a transitional stage; for others, it was a stage of development in which they became stuck. And for those fellowships that grew into churches, the youthful, headstrong spirit of fellowship culture often caused difficulties, as described in the next chapter, "Becoming Churches."

Churches, Sects and Fellowships

Many aspects of fellowship culture reflect the differences between sects and churches. These differences were explored in depth by early 20th-century German theologian and sociologist Ernst Troeltsch in his groundbreaking work, *The Social Teachings of the Christian Churches.*

According to Troeltsch, sects are usually experimental, sometimes radical, and fairly fluid as their beliefs and practices evolve. In contrast, churches—meaning denominations, in this sense of the term—are established entities with clearly defined beliefs, practices, and behavior. A church is usually a sect that has matured into something settled and predictable. To some, this stability is boring, repetitious, and stifling. To others, it offers comfort and structure. Within a particular church tradition, a visitor from another congregation will find a predictable order of service and familiar teachings, holidays, and symbols.

Sects can appear anywhere along the spectrum of belief, but are found most often at the two extremes: the very conservative and the very liberal. American religious culture in the last two centuries has created a number of such sects. Mormons (Church of Jesus Christ of Latter-day Saints), Jehovah's Witnesses, and Christian Scientists are members of well-known sects in the United States that have evolved into large religious movements with a churchlike character. These sects exist alongside such non-Christian movements as Scientology and Wicca. Sects can also be found in other major religious traditions, including Judaism and Islam. Unitarianism originated as one of many new Christian sects in the Radical Reformation—the left wing of the 16th-century Reformation—which also generated such groups as the Schwenkenfelders, the Mennonites, and the Anabaptists. Christianity itself originated as a sect within first-century Judaism and took three centuries to become a church.

Many sects withdraw from the larger society in order to remain pure. The Amish and the Mennonites are among the groups that have chosen that route. Other sects continue to engage both the larger society and the established church in hopes of purifying or renewing them. That engagement may be evangelical, with members aggressively seeking more converts, as the Mormons and the Jehovah's Witnesses do. Or it may take place within the church, the paths originally chosen by both the Methodists and the Puritans. In either case, the defining characteristics of most sects are energy, enthusiasm, and willingness to innovate (or in the case of a conservative sect, to "de-innovate"). If a sect succeeds in attracting many followers, it is likely to evolve into a church in its own right. If that happens, some of that vitality becomes institutionalized.

Compared to other sects, the lay-led fellowship movement in Unitarianism is unique. It is the only case in which the denomination essentially authorized, and even sponsored, the creation of a sect within the existing church. That uneasy relationship between the institutional and the anti-institutional lies at the heart of the fellowship story. In retrospect, fellowship culture was an inevitable outcome of a strategy of turning laypersons loose to create their own religious movement, then attempting to integrate them back into the larger movement that had spawned them. Nearly 60 years after the beginning of the fellowship era, that reintegration has been fairly successful, but not without bumps in the road and residual after-effects of the sect experience.

Voluntary Associations and Fellowships

Both churches and lay-led fellowships belong to the broader category of nongovernmental organizations, or NGOs—organizations that are neither family nor business nor government. NGOs encompass everything from labor unions and colleges to the local humane society. NGOs that originate locally and are run by volunteers—such as fellowships—were of particular interest to James Luther Adams, one of the most distinguished Unitarian theologians of the 20th century. Adams traced these voluntary associations, like sects, to the Radical Reformation. In a 1962 address, he described their characteristics this way:

> The voluntary association at its best offers an institutional framework within which the give and take of discussion may be promoted, an institutional framework within which consensus or practice may be brought under criticism and be subjected to change. It offers a means for bringing a variety of perspectives into interplay. It offers a means for breaking through old social structures in order to meet new needs. It is a means of dispersing power, in the sense that power is the capacity to participate in making social decisions. It is the

> training ground of the skills that are required for viable social existence in a democracy. In short, the voluntary association is a means for the institutionalizing of gradual revolution.

That description sounds like a recipe for a lay-led fellowship!

Sociologists have found that relatively few people participate in voluntary associations that promote the general welfare rather than serve a special interest group. Churches are an exception, whether they promote individual salvation, work for social justice, or both. A passion for making the world a better place has long been characteristic of both Unitarianism and Universalism. But to an even greater extent than traditional congregations, lay-led fellowships exhibit an evangelistic fervor for creating the kingdom of heaven on earth and faith in their ability to actually do so.

Many of the people attracted to Unitarian Universalism, and in particular to fellowships, were looking at least in part for institutions through which they could practice what Troeltsch called the "objective virtues." These are public virtues, rather than those acted on in interpersonal encounters. Objective virtues are expressed in social justice work. They are almost impossible to practice outside a community of like-minded individuals. The teaching and shared expression of the objective virtues is a major focus of liberal religion in general and Unitarian Universalism in particular. Most fellowships shared with the larger religious movement a genuine passion for justice work of many kinds—economic, social, political, environmental, and racial. In a small group, unencumbered by the responsibilities of a building, staff, and sometimes even religious education, and with a great deal of freedom in defining their purpose, lay-led fellowships could easily find common ground and a unifying principle in some social cause.

But fellowship culture cannot simply be defined by enthusiastic social justice organizing. In congregational visits, interviews with UUA staff members, and the writings of others who have studied the fellowship movement, certain characteristics of fellowship culture emerge again and again. They can be grouped into four common themes:

- Worship style—A preference for an informal, highly intellectual, and highly participatory (sometimes even combative) worship style. Many fellowships and former fellowships resist organization and structure in the worship service, and often in other aspects of congregational life as well.
- "Flat-earth" humanism—This somewhat tongue-in-cheek label refers to a highly humanistic theology that shows the same intolerance toward other theological understandings that one observes in fundamentalists on the opposite end of the religious spectrum.
- Resistance to growth—An ambivalent attitude toward newcomers and a reluctance to increase membership. Expressed more positively, many fellowships prefer to remain small and intimate.
- Resistance to authority—A negative or ambivalent attitude toward any kind of authority, but particularly clergy and the UUA. In many cases, this attitude is coupled with a lack of a historic sense of connection to the larger faith movement.

Not every congregation that began as a lay-led fellowship has all four of these elements. (Resistance to growth, in particular, was present in some congregations but not others.) And congregations of more traditional origin may have some of the same characteristics. But taken together, these four elements generally characterize fellowship culture. They also help explain some of the growing pains of lay-led fellowships as they encounter new challenges. The smaller and more isolated the congregation, the more likely it was to exhibit all four elements to a marked degree. The rest of this chapter will examine each element in turn.

Worship Style

Probably no issue generates more heated responses among members of fellowships than what happens when the community gathers on Sunday morning. A note to Munroe Husbands, director of the Fellowship Office, from the Galveston County Fellowship in Texas in the early 1950s describes the challenge faced by lay-led fellowships in organizing the Sunday service:

> Chief among our problems has been the one of offering a type of service which will satisfy both the theists and the humanists among us. At the moment we seem to have attained a temporary truce, and we hope for happy relationships from now on. To this end, we have substituted unison for responsive reading, take no collection from our congregation, and have no music other than that selectively chosen for our recorder by [one of the members]. The hymns are read: baskets for contributions are placed on a table near the entrance door.

Even today, many fellowships struggle with worship—including the word itself. (Many prefer *service* or even *program*, believing that worship requires an object or God.) Perhaps the term *worship* creates such discomfort because fellowships tend to attract a large number of unchurched persons, as well as refugees from other religious traditions. That mix of newcomers—some fleeing congregations where they felt suppressed, others unfamiliar with the normal protocols of churches—probably accounts for many aspects of fellowship culture.

Fellowships find their own ways to worship. Some will pray, many do not; more will sing, but some do not. Some have a structured order of service with elements repeated each week, while others resist any trappings of ritual in their Sunday morning gatherings. One might describe this resistance to ritual as a remnant of the Protestant Reformation's reaction against the highly ritualized Catholic mass.

One contemporary lay-led fellowship with 50 members describes itself on its web site as

> a lay-led, welcoming congregation with services that are religious only in the broadest sense. Rather, our services celebrate the merged streams of ethical and moral concepts which characterize our increasingly multicultural society, provide learning opportunities, and discuss local environmental and community issues. Time for congregational response and feedback is scheduled and an atmosphere of informality prevails.

At a large number of lay-led fellowships, two elements in particular are characteristic of the Sunday morning gathering. One is a refusal to pass an offering plate as part of the service. While researching her book *Bright Galaxy* in the late 1950s, Laile Bartlett found that she could almost invariably evoke a strong response by asking whether the fellowship passed the plate. Fifty years later, some congregations that began as lay-led fellowships still do not pass an offering plate. Instead, they invite contributions in other ways, such as a conspicuous container at the back of the room or a reminder in the Sunday bulletin.

The other element found in the worship services of many fellowships is *talkback*, a congregational response to the sermon within or immediately after the service. In some congregations the practice is called *dialogue*, *conversation*, or *sermon response*. Whatever its name, this fellowship invention has found its way into more traditional congregations and is now widespread in Unitarian Universalism, and even among some liberal congregations in other denominations.

Flat-Earth Humanism

During the formative period of the fellowship movement, humanism was the dominant theological position among Unitarians. Thus, one might expect fellowships to favor humanist theology.

But why did so many of them adopt the intolerant viewpoint known as "flat-earth" humanism—a fundamentalism of the left that resisted, or even derided, any notion of God, spirituality, or religious experience? The answer lies partly in psychology and partly in the atmosphere of the times.

Many newcomers to Unitarianism came from a Christian background that was fairly dogmatic. In particular, many had belonged to denominations wedded to biblical inerrancy or in the throes of the neo-orthodoxy of the mid-twentieth century. At the same time, they had come of age intellectually and religiously under the influence of the humanist movement. They were willing to question everything, including whether their congregation was part of a religion and whether the word "sacred" still held any meaning. According to anthropologist Mircea Eliade,

> Religious man . . . always believes that there is an absolute reality, the sacred, which transcends this world but manifests itself in this world, thereby sanctifying it and making it real . . . The non-religious man refuses transcendence, accepts the relativity of "reality," and may even come to doubt the meaning of existence. . . . Man makes himself, and he only makes himself completely in proportion as he desacralizes himself and the world. The sacred is the prime obstacle to his freedom.

Any extreme force tends to produce its opposite. Thus resisting religious dogma often results in an equally strong mirror image of the rejected position. "Flat-earth" humanism, which can be as dogmatic as the Christian orthodoxy it rejects, is a prime example. O'Neal describes this posture as adolescent—pushing away to gain independence under the false impression that the newly adopted stance is an original creation rather than a reaction. Such an attitude also reveals an ignorance of history. Many fellowship members know little of Unitarianism's long and complex history within Christianity and how that experience has shaped it as a religious movement. They think of their fellowship, and fellowships in general, as having sprung into existence independently, wholly new and original.

The battle between the two fundamentalist viewpoints, religious and humanist, is not just about theology; it is also about the clash between the forces of authority and autonomy. When these two forces are in opposition, the normal resolution is to make space for both. But in this case, each brand of fundamentalism takes an extreme position. Christian fundamentalists take the authoritarian extreme. Humanist fundamentalists are equally entrenched on the opposite end of the spectrum: autonomy at any cost.

The revolt against the structure and trappings of institutional religion, along with other dimensions of fellowship culture, was in part a product of the culture in which these congregations emerged and grew to adolescence. The 1950s were marked by a perceived conformity and blandness of culture, captured in such books about popular culture as David Riesman's *The Lonely Crowd* and William Whyte's *The Organization Man*. The reaction to the cultural insipidness of the 1950s was the rise of the counterculture in the 1960s—a decade of intense social activism, from the civil rights movement to antiwar protests to feminist consciousness-raising. These two decades, which coincided with the fellowship movement, provided a cultural context of revolt, experimentation, and intense individualism. Those who joined fellowships felt like they were casting off an oppressive history and creating something new and unique, not just in fellowships but in the larger Unitarian and Universalist movements, and indeed in the larger society.

As the culture reacted against the excesses of the 1960s in the decades that followed, so did Unitarian Universalism. The faith movement largely recovered its respect for the sacred, for transcendent experience, and for expressing dimensions of being other than the intellectual. Still, an attachment to humanism and a resistance to conventional forms of worship persist, to some degree, in many congregations formed as lay-led fellowships.

One visible residue of that history in a number of congregations is the practice of holding humanist forums as an alternative

Sunday morning service. Many fellowships held similar forums in the early days. (In the Las Vegas, Nevada, congregation, a forum was held from the 1960s to the early 1980s on Friday nights, fondly remembered by some as "Friday Night Fights.")

At the Sunday morning forums that still persist, those who long for the "good old days" can gather with like-minded newer members for an informal discussion centered on a book or a topic. A typical forum features lively give and take with none of the trappings of worship—no hymns, no readings, no meditation or prayer, no language of spirituality.

In the Athens, Georgia, congregation, for example, 30 or 40 people gather at 9:30 on Sunday morning to listen to a speaker, then engage in discussion. Most of the forum members stay for coffee and mingle with the larger congregation as it gathers for the 11 a.m. service. Many will then leave before the service, satisfied by their particular form of Sunday worship. Similar humanist gatherings take place in other congregations as well, including Stillwater, Oklahoma; Carbondale, Illinois; and Topeka, Kansas.

One fairly large midwestern fellowship with a long and contentious attachment to lay leadership reserved the prime time 11 a.m. service for the humanist style of worship, relegating the more traditional, "spiritual" service to 9:15 a.m. They were surprised to find that the earlier service—in spite of being inconvenient for parents with children in religious education—attracted a strong following among newcomers. Apparently the newer members were less enamored of the humanist approach than the longtime members were.

Newcomers and Growth

Another aspect of fellowship culture—the reluctance to grow—is widely perceived as a problem. Laile Bartlett saw it differently. She recognized no mandate for small fellowships to grow; in her view, a congregation could choose to remain small and intimate. It is easy to do that simply by not being highly visible. One Florida congregation we visited was so hard to find that we had to be led there by a combination of cell phone directions and a person standing at a corner waving! This congregation is puzzled, but not particularly disturbed, by its failure to grow.

Why do so many fellowships resist growth? Many simply feel an attachment to small size, ownership, and intimacy as part of their religious experience. A small congregation meets those needs in a way that a larger one might not. Small groups allow each person more time and space for self-expression. They make it possible for members to know each other more intimately and foster a greater sensitivity to differences of opinion. They also create a stronger sense of responsibility for being present and fully participating, as well as more opportunities to assume leadership roles. Today many larger congregations are actively seeking to restore these qualities through small group ministry programs, such as covenant groups.

Another reason for not wanting to grow may be resistance to the changes and financial responsibilities that growth brings. As a congregation grows larger, it eventually needs to acquire a building and a minister. Both cost money. At the same time, both result in greater visibility, which in turn leads to still more growth. The need to pay for programs, services, staff, and buildings generates additional pressure to bring in more and more new members. For a small fellowship, the prospect of this endless spiral of growth may seem daunting.

On the other hand, small size has disadvantages. The intimacy that some people find attractive may be a drawback for those who want anonymity or simply prefer the experience of worshipping in a larger group. More significantly, the life of a small fellowship can be precarious. Overworked leaders often burn out. Loss of even a single member can exact a high cost, especially if that person was a major contributor or a valued leader. There may not be a critical mass for religious education classes, a choir, or other programs that members desire.

At the heart of the issue regarding size, however, are the attitudes toward growth of Unitarian Universalism as a whole. Any faith tradition that believes it has something to offer—whether it is salvation, wisdom, insight, or values—normally wants to attract individuals and make its voice heard. Unitarian Universalism is not a proselytizing faith; it freely acknowledges the validity of many spiritual paths and offers its own path simply as one among many. But to the extent that there are people seeking what this faith has to offer, Unitarian Universalists have an obligation to try to meet that need through both new and existing congregations.

Lay-led fellowships, as part of the larger faith community, share the obligation to welcome the stranger. They must be willing to accept newcomers graciously and integrate them into the life of the congregation, even if it increases their size beyond the comfort zone.

There is no perfect size for a congregation, or indeed for any voluntary community. The important thing for any congregation is to carry out the mission appropriate for its own size, location, and stage of development. Small congregations without much growth potential have a place in this movement as faithful witnesses to liberal religion. At the same time, larger or growing congregations need to be aware of the need for smaller circles of intimacy.

Religious faith is not a private matter. If Unitarian Universalism wishes to bring about the kingdom of God on earth, to work for social justice and environmental responsibility from within a faith community and exert some influence on others, every congregation must remain open to the possibility of change and growth.

Attitudes Toward Clergy

Resistance to authority is the fourth element commonly found among congregations that began as fellowships. The "flat-earth" humanism discussed earlier is one example of opposition to institutional authority. But it can also take other forms such as libertarianism, an anticlerical attitude, or just a frontier mentality of going it alone and liking it.

The Unitarian Universalist faith tradition has a strongly libertarian streak that coexists uneasily with the need to affiliate with like-minded others. Fellowship culture reflects that aspect of Unitarian Universalism; in fact, fellowships often bring out the inner libertarian in their members. One minister to a former fellowship speculated that fellowships attract people with a need or desire to be in charge.

Unitarian Universalists are also, by and large, well educated. For some, being educated means respecting fellow professionals, such as clergy or denominational staff, and valuing their contribution to the larger enterprise. For others, being educated can mean rejecting any external authority, regardless of training, credentials, or experience.

Resistance to authority often extends to distrust of denominational leadership. In our site visits, many fellowship members expressed a mixture of disdain, ignorance, and indifference to the Unitarian Universalist Association. UUA headquarters—or "Boston," as it is often referred to—is seen as a place where congregations send large fair share payments and receive little in return, except for occasional useful services such as books and religious education curricula. Although attitudes toward their districts are generally more positive, many fellowships, particularly those far from Boston, do not think of themselves as part of a larger movement.

Another side effect of libertarian attitudes, especially when combined with small size, can be an excess of democracy. In some fellowships, everyone insists on having a voice in every decision, however small. Governance operates as a committee of the whole. Members are reluctant to entrust decision-making authority not only to the minister (if they have one), but even to their elected lay leaders. In such circumstances, congregational meetings are likely to be frequent, contentious, and prolonged.

Like some other elements of fellowship culture, resistance to authority is a negative that arises from a positive. Empowering the laity is commendable. It allows congregation members to experience the joys and responsibilities of ownership. It reflects the

Protestant heritage of both the Unitarian and Universalist faith traditions, a heritage that at its best honors the priesthood (and in the words of James Luther Adams, the prophethood) of all believers. Empowering laypersons means that members are not just allowed, but also expected to take responsibility for their own spiritual life.

But as part of a community, laypersons must also learn to share responsibility and work together to reach common goals. That is never more true than when a lay-led fellowship hires its first minister—one of the many challenges it faces on the journey toward becoming a church.

Most surviving first-wave fellowships have had some experience with professional ministry. They might start with part-time, consulting, or temporary ministry. But the majority have found a way to partner with a full-time, ordained minister on a long-term basis. A good ministerial experience can result in a more positive attitude toward clergy authority.

Often, however, the first settlement was a bumpy ride for both minister and congregation. One minister to a former lay-led fellowship joked that "Unitarian fellowships don't need Jesus, they get to crucify their first minister!"

Many people who joined lay-led fellowships were refugees from bad experiences with authoritarian clergy and authoritarian traditions. They often expected to have similarly negative experiences with Unitarian or Unitarian Universalist ministers—and in some cases, they were right. A number of early lay-led fellowships recruited their first ministers on their own, instead of going through the denomination. Ordaining a lay minister from among their own members was a common practice. In other cases, a fellowship might choose someone who had never completed the ordination process, came from a different faith tradition, or had failed at one or more previous settlements. When those relationships soured, as many did, it set back the cause of professional ministry in those congregations for a long time.

But even when fellowships found a minister through a more discerning process or with the assistance of the denomination, they still faced a difficult adjustment. The largest challenge was a simple one. As long as a congregation remained lay-led, power and leadership were the sole province of the members. By granting power to a minister, the members reduced their own power. In other words, authority was often viewed as a fixed pie, a zero-sum game in which the minister's gain means a corresponding loss to lay leaders.

In other cases, fellowships welcomed the minister as someone to take the burden of responsibility off the shoulders of a few overworked, exhausted lay leaders. Ministers could find themselves expected to do anything and everything. One minister, new to a formerly lay-led congregation in the South, was asked if she did windows! Clearly, learning to share leadership, authority, and responsibility is a challenge to all parties involved. We will explore some of these transitional experiences in the next chapter.

Becoming Churches

In the first ten years of the fellowship movement, 29 congregations made the leap from fellowship to church—seven of them in 1954 alone. For these groups and the many others that followed, becoming a church was not a simple matter. It was a journey that required changes in size, in leadership, in responsibilities, and in self-understanding. Each congregation had to navigate the path from being a small, close-knit group to a larger, welcoming community; from lay leadership to shared leadership with a minister; from limited financial responsibilities to supporting a building and staff; and from a high degree of informality to a more structured worship service and program of ministry.

When the fellowship program was created in 1947, very little thought was given to how these transitions would be financed and guided. The results were mixed. A few congregations made the leap to church status so quickly that they barely recall their fellowship origins. Many more, however, went through long and painful transitions. Still others got stuck at some size or stage of the process.

The American Unitarian Association had long provided financial support for the formation of new congregations. But its policies and programs were designed to help grow only a few new churches a year. Having planted seeds for so many new fellowships, the AUA now faced harvesting a bumper crop that threatened to strain its limited resources. New strategies were needed to accommodate the new reality.

One of the first steps was to rethink the requirements for acceptance into the AUA as a church. Originally, at least 50 member families were needed for a congregation to be eligible. In 1955 a provision was added for fellowships, requiring a minimum size of only ten members. At the same time, the minimum size for a church was increased. Under the revised standards, a church required at least 65 resident, contributing families, as well as a surrounding community with the potential for further growth. (Sometimes the minimum size requirement was relaxed if the growth potential in the community was especially strong.) In addition, the congregation's budget had to be sufficient to pay the salary of a full-time resident minister.

Although a formal name change was not one of the requirements, the AUA did expect congregations to change their name from *fellowship* to *church* when they officially reached church status. The intent was to preserve a clear distinction between the two types of organizations. Huntington, on Long Island, was one of the first to rebel and insist on keeping its "maiden" name. In some cases, resistance to the word *church* was an effort to retain an independent identity. But it also respected the feelings of individuals who found that word uncomfortable or even painful, as humanists, people with a Jewish background, and refugees from very conservative Christianity often did. Eventually Boston relented. Today there are congregations with over 500 members and multiple clergy staff that still carry the word *fellowship* in their name, such as the Eno River Fellowship in Chapel Hill, North Carolina. There is also a trend toward using other designations, such as *society*, *community*, or *congregation*, in lieu of *church*.

The initiative to make the transition from fellowship to church could be encouraged from without, but ultimately the commitment had to come from within. As discussed in the previous chapter, fellowship culture is often resistant to growth. It is easy for a congregation to become invested in intimacy, lay ownership, and a particular operating style. External pressure to grow will not succeed if there is no commitment to do so within the group.

Once a fellowship makes a commitment to grow, it must decide which to do first: acquire a building or call a minister. The order varies from one congregation to another, and the gap between the first step and the second can be quite long. The Clemson, South Carolina, congregation, established in 1954, constructed a building in 1979 and occupied it for 18 years before calling a minister. On the other hand, the congregation in San Luis Obispo, California, established in 1952, called its first minister in the late 1970s and did not acquire its first building until 1989.

Fellowship Office director Munroe Husbands generally recommended purchasing or constructing a building first—primarily to serve the needs of religious education, but also to give the group stability and permanence. Other congregations called a minister first, hoping that this step would lead to the kind of growth that would make a building financially feasible. Other than passing the plate, no single issue has generated more controversy among fellowships in transition than which major step to take first.

Creative Housing

Those that chose the "building first" strategy did so for a variety of reasons. Some had no intention of ever calling a minister, at least not in their planning horizon. Some, particularly those with an active religious education program, were simply too crowded in their current rented space. Others had trouble securing or retaining rented quarters, especially in areas where they were viewed as radical. Still other congregations thought that they would have a better chance of attracting a good minister if they had a satisfactory physical space, including a worship center, offices for the minister and administrator, and spaces for religious education and social gatherings.

Many congregations that needed to buy or build a space of their own were aided by the Extension Department, which offered loans up to a maximum of $8,000, with repayment periods of six to seven years and very low interest rates.

For congregations that could not afford to build or buy right away, sometimes shared space was the answer. The congregation in Falmouth, Massachusetts, shared space with a Quaker congregation for 29 years, meeting at different hours. Many congregations have found a synagogue a satisfactory housing partner, in part because the Jewish Sabbath is on Saturday, but also because Jewish congregations are sometimes more philosophically and theologically congenial than traditional Christian churches.

Another common solution was to buy and remodel a house, although most congregations that chose this route outgrew it quickly. Even homes with large living-dining areas have limited capacity for worship and social gatherings. Kitchens designed for families do not always work well for larger groups; bedrooms are often too small and too few for offices and religious education classrooms. Parking is usually inadequate as well.

Morristown, New Jersey, bought and remodeled a three-story mansion. Franklin, North Carolina, occupies a house that has been remodeled to accommodate their needs, but is preparing to build a more "church-like" building on the same site. Bellport (formerly Brookhaven) on Long Island purchased a house built in 1857 that has had many additions, including porches, a ballroom (now the sanctuary), and a carriage house.

Houses are just one of many options. The Troy, Michigan, congregation occupies a converted barn that is on the National Register of Historic Places. Cheyenne, Wyoming, occupies a former Latter-day Saints church building. Santa Rosa, California, may win the prize for the most novel collection of buildings. They started out holding services at a mortuary, with religious education classes in a Teamsters union hall. They later moved to an old school. Currently, the congregation occupies a former multiplex theater in downtown Santa Rosa.

Ministerial Challenges

As fellowships grew in size, it became inevitable that they would not only construct buildings but consider the need for professional leadership. Some began with a director of religious education. But most fellowships called a minister as their first professional staff.

Professional clerical leadership is important not only for the local congregation, but for the larger denomination. As one UU minister noted,

> Fellowships are much more likely to be vital centers of liberal religious activity with ministerial leadership. The absence of a leader who is familiar with UU heritage, the power of ritual, and an understanding of prayer and worship leads inevitably to a congregation with a shallow or no connection to the wider Unitarian movement [other] than in name.

While clergy may have seen the need for professional leadership, fellowships did not always see it the same way. Carbondale, Illinois, founded in 1952, holds the record for the greatest number of years between its founding and calling a clergyperson. It was lay-led for 47 years before seeking a minister in 1999. The longer a congregation remained lay-led, the more difficult the transition to professional ministry was likely to be—for the minister as well as the congregation.

In an April 1961 memo, Richard Gibbs, director of the AUA Extension Department, addressed some of the concerns reported by the first ministers of new churches, most of which had been lay-led fellowships. A common complaint was that lay leaders failed to consult the minister when appropriate. Members often had negative stereotypes of ministers based on experiences with clergy from other churches. Some ministers were undermined by "snipers" from the losing anticlerical faction. Much of the conflict focused on the format and content of the Sunday service.

After interviewing ministers, laypersons, and denominational officials while researching the fellowship movement, Rev. Dan

O'Neal observed that fellowships generally did not start out as anticlerical, but "their subsequent years of independence tended to create tensions around eventual ministerial leadership." Fellowships that arose as splinter groups from established churches were most likely to take an anti-clerical stance. Those that emerged as friendly spin-offs, supported and even sponsored by established churches, were more likely to think kindly of ministers.

Fellowship culture created challenges for the ministers interviewed by O'Neal, in varying degrees of intensity. Issues of clerical authority, the structure of the Sunday morning service, and "flat-earth" humanism were common. Some ministers also faced battles over resistance to growth, religious education, and engagement in social action. Many encountered a resistance to ritual of any kind and a refusal to engage in theological dialogue.

In 1962, twelve ministers and ten laypersons, all from formerly lay-led fellowships in the West, gathered in California to discuss the challenges they experienced as their congregations transitioned from lay leadership to ministerial leadership. The report from that meeting, titled "Under the Palms," was an honest and thoughtful description of those struggles. It also offered some lessons to help other fellowships anticipate problems and resolve them effectively. The questions addressed in the report were:

- Whether the fellowship form itself gave rise to anti-clerical attitudes
- Whether the image of a minister to which fellowship members reacted had any validity when applied to Unitarian Universalist ministers
- Whether fellowship members were willing to make space for a minister to find something satisfying or meaningful to do
- Whether ministers were willing to adapt to the culture of strong lay leadership they often encountered

While all of these issues arose in many congregations, by far the most significant were the last two.

Some key lessons emerged from this conversation and others like it around the country. The participants agreed that the advent of a minister was likely to result in a struggle for control. Fellowships were not adequately prepared for sharing leadership with ministers, and ministers with traditional seminary training were not prepared for what they encountered in fellowships.

A fellowship's lay leaders, having birthed their religious community and raised it to a kind of adulthood, felt a strong sense of ownership. This clashed with the minister's desire to shape the worship and ministry of the congregation. Sometimes it took a second or even a third minister before a fellowship settled into a workable arrangement of shared ministry.

Some of the ministers at the "Under the Palms" meeting recounted very difficult experiences. The fellowships often found it hard to work in partnership with a minister, to accept the value of the minister's training and experience, and to see themselves as part of a larger religious movement. In the less successful ministerial placements, the minister was regarded as an interloper, a self-proclaimed authority figure, a threat to the traditions of the community and the power of lay leaders. From the clergy perspective, such congregations paid lip service to democracy and shared ministry while under the surface, an oligarchy of entrenched leadership protected its turf.

From the layperson's perspective, there were concerns—often justified—about the minister taking too much of the leadership of the congregation. The reluctance of lay leaders to surrender control led to the widespread practice of limiting the minister to preaching two Sundays a month. Huntington, Long Island, held to that standard from its first called minister in the 1950s until 2004, when its new minister was granted pulpit privileges for two Sundays out of three.

Although lay worship leaders were reluctant to surrender the pulpit, often they were willing to be coached in worship leadership by the minister. The concept of coaching could extend to other aspects of the minister's role as well. In the fellowships that adapted most easily, lay leaders viewed the minister as a partner, guide, and teacher rather than an authority figure.

Calling a minister was expected to lead to growth, and it often did. But along with growth came challenges, such as integrating newcomers, adapting programs to a larger group, and coping with the discomfort of change. In many fellowships, it was easier to blame these "problems" on the minister than accept them as inevitable side effects of growth.

According to the participants whose experiences were described in "Under the Palms," fellowships looked for their first minister to fill certain roles. These included representation in the larger community, leadership in developing the religious education program, and pastoral counseling. Preaching was initially less important to most fellowships. Above all, participants agreed, a successful minister in this transitional role needed to be flexible, adaptable, and respectful of the traditions that were developed prior to his or her arrival.

In a 1955 memo, Munroe Husbands identified the critical qualifications for ministers serving congregations transitioning from fellowship to church status. First, the ministers must be experienced and of proven ability, since they represent the church to the community (particularly if there is no building). They must be prepared to deal with members who are new to Unitarianism and who are theologically diverse. To cope with the challenges of fellowship culture, the ministers must avoid dogmatism or authoritarianism. They must be flexible, trust in congregational polity, coordinate scattered activities, and build a sense of "churchmanship"—all while managing the perceived threat to established lay leadership. These tasks are not for the faint of heart, the inexperienced, or those deeply invested in ministerial authority!

Extension director Gibbs's 1961 memo on problems faced by ministers took another look at the same question. Gibbs concluded that the first minister to a fellowship needed to be permissive and flexible rather than authoritarian, and that the personality of the minister was the key to a successful transition.

In 1956, in response to some fellowships' poor choices, the AUA board of directors set guidelines for calling ministers to fellowships. Fellowships were urged to consult about candidates with the regional director (predecessor to the district executive), the fellowship director (Munroe Husbands), and the director of the Department of Ministry. In general, the guidelines advised, a candidate should have experience in parish ministry and knowledge of the denomination and its history, be a capable preacher, and be able to offer leadership in other areas such as religious education, public relations, and personal counseling.

In addition to the difficulties of ministerial transitions, congregations and the AUA faced a shortage of ministers for emerging churches. Over the years, several strategies for addressing both issues were employed with varying success. These strategies included the minister-at-large program, student ministers, visiting clergy, the ministers-on-loan program, and extension ministry.

The Minister-at-Large Program

Prior to the fellowship program, the principal strategy for helping emerging groups prepare for professional ministry was to send the minister-at-large. Lon Ray Call served in this capacity until 1950, when he was called to full-time parish ministry at the South Nassau Fellowship. In 1956, the Extension Department reinstated the minister-at-large program with Rev. Grant Butler. Butler assisted two congregations a year for three months each as they moved from fellowship status to church status. He served as minister-at-large until his death in 1967. During that period he would serve as a full-time minister, preaching regularly, working with the leadership and helping them develop strategies for growth in membership and financial support.

In general, a fellowship was more likely to receive the services of the minister-at-large if it had an annual budget of at least $2,500 and 45 contributing family units, as well as a meeting place and a religious education program. The fellowship had to agree to work toward achieving the minimum size for church status (65 resident member families) and calling a minister.

In 1959, Butler wrote an evaluation of the minister-at-large program. He felt that the primary goal of the program was to build membership rather than solve problems or resolve conflicts. The AUA intended this service to be a tool to help fellowships call ministers and become churches. Because of the cost of the program, as well as the limited number of ministers available, Butler argued that the minister-at-large program should be limited to those fellowships that showed the greatest promise of becoming churches. Even that recommendation fell by the wayside. Butler's death in 1967 marked the end of the minister-at-large program.

Student Ministers

In the early 1950s, the Fellowship Office experimented with a summer student minister program. The goal was to provide low-cost, short-term ministerial services to fellowships prior to them committing to settled ministry.

A 1953 report on five such placements (in Chattanooga, Galveston, Jacksonville, Paducah, and Shreveport) reveals some interesting challenges. Some of the student ministers faced the problem of small, discouraged congregations that needed to be revived. Many seminarians struggled to adjust to the different expectations for the Sunday service. Most fellowships had little awareness of the larger movement and the difference between a church and a debating society. At least three of the fellowships were eager for the student minister to help them grow and later reported disappointment that more growth did not occur. In a few instances, the student minister helped create or reshape the children's religious education program. After this initial experiment, the Fellowship Office student minister program lapsed.

However, the Fellowship Office program was not the only way in which student ministers served fellowships. Some congregations, especially those located near seminaries, provided a pulpit in which ministerial students honed their preaching skills. At least two fellowships elected to "grow" their own ministers by helping to fund divinity school education for members of their congregation. In return, those members served their congregations as student ministers while they completed their studies. Central Square in New York and Athens, Ohio, (and possibly other congregations as well) chose this route as an affordable transition to professional ministry.

Ministers-on-Loan and Visiting Ministers

Another strategy for preparing congregations to call ministers of their own was the minister-on-loan program. An established congregation would agree to loan its minister to an emerging congregation for six weeks or so. During that time, the minister-on-loan would conduct services, work with leaders, take steps to build membership and visibility, and try to solve various problems. This was a low-cost approach to helping fellowships. The cost fell largely on the minister's home congregation, which agreed to pay his or her salary during the loan period. The UUA paid travel costs and some other limited expenses. In the height of the fellowship period and beyond, the minister-on-loan program, begun in the 1940s, became an increasingly valuable tool for helping fellowships get past plateaus and explore professional ministry.

The minister-on-loan was not necessarily from the immediate area. In one long-distance loan, Arthur Wilmot, minister of the Corvallis, Oregon, congregation served the Falmouth, Massachusetts, fellowship in February and March of 1988.

Ames, Iowa, one of the first five fellowships to be formed (in 1948), went through two minister-on-loan experiences before calling a full-time minister in 1987. However, not all minister-on-loan programs succeeded in preparing the congregation for full-time ministry. Greeley, Colorado, participated in the program in the 1980s, but has never had more than part-time ministry and is currently lay-led.

If a fellowship could not obtain a minister-on-loan or some other form of transitional minister, it could have the benefit of clergy presence on at least some Sundays by extending an invitation to visiting ministers. Typically, fellowships tried to schedule visiting clergy to occupy the pulpit once a month or so, if any were available within a reasonable distance. Some fellowships developed relationships with one or more area ministers who supplied their pulpit on a regular basis as an alternative to the more frequent lay-led services. This kind of exposure to professional ministry often helped overcome fears and stereotypes of ministers as authority figures.

Extension Ministry

With the closure of the Fellowship Office and the onset of financial difficulties in the late 1960s, the UUA put on hold the funding of ministerial transitions for fellowships. But as money from the Veatch Foundation became available in the early 1970s (see "The End of an Experiment"), support for fellowships in transition once again became financially possible. The minister-on-loan program was still the priority at the time, but this was a short-term effort. Something more lasting was needed to stem the high mortality rate of fellowships that tried to make the transition to full-fledged churches.

Initiated in 1977, the extension ministry program was intended to help lay-led fellowships that were ready for a minister but remained unable to fully fund one themselves. After applying to the program, an eligible congregation would be matched with a minister who had been through specialized training. This training prepared the minister to focus on growth and to anticipate the adjustments that the congregation was likely to experience. The program subsidized part of the extension minister's salary for several years (at first five, later three). The goal was for the congregation to be financially able to support a minister on its own by the end of the extension period. It could then call the extension minister as a settled minister if it chose to do so.

The extension ministry program lasted 25 years. During that time, 133 extension ministers were placed, mainly in congregations that started as lay-led fellowships. (Some congregations in the program, like the one in Auburn, Maine, were established churches that needed help to recover from decline.) In the later years of the program, the criteria for eligibility became more stringent and more emphasis was placed on preparing both the congregation and the minister for the transition experience. The extension ministry program ended in 2004, after the number of eligible congregations applying had declined to only one or two a year.

With the aid of extension training, and the "bribe" of transitional support, many of the later transitions to professional ministry were less painful than those in the 1960s and 1970s. Cynthia Prescott offers this first-hand account of her positive transition experience as the first minister to Clemson, South Carolina, which had an exceptionally long lay-led history:

> I once declared grandly to seminary classmates in a course on congregational life that I would never move to the South and never agree to become the first minister in a formerly lay-led fellowship. Within the year following graduation I had done both those things at once. Ten years on, here I am, still serving the Unitarian Universalist Fellowship of Clemson, South Carolina. Not only have I lived to rue my seminary remark, mainly by laughing at it, but I've also lived to learn how deeply I have been blessed by what in retrospect really was a big risk for a newly-minted minister to have taken. The fellowship had not been "ministered" since its founding in 1954. I had never *been* a minister before coming to Clemson. I arrived in 1998. Mutual innocence, occasionally crossing the border into mutual ignorance, made the fellowship and me a suitable fit—or at least more tolerant of one another's fumblings and foibles—a tolerance that thankfully endures to this day.

The congregational environment often referred to as "fellowship culture" is commonly described as unfriendly to structure, planning, growth, theological diversity, and most of all, to clergy leadership. Without a doubt, there's truth in that image, as a number of my colleagues can testify first-hand. However, what attracted me to the Clemson fellowship was the congregation's lively, inventive approach to worship; lots of capable, self-directed lay leadership; and an authentically warm community, housed in a spacious, comfortable building on well-tended grounds. In the trips we made to research this book, I saw those same features repeated in congregations small and not-so-small anymore, all of which began as lay-led fellowships.

The Districts Take Charge

In the mid-1960s, the Extension Department shifted a significant portion of the responsibility for supporting lay-led fellowships to regional directors. A 1966 memo outlines the responsibilities of the Boston office and the districts. The UUA would continue to help with funding (until 1967, when it switched to the districts), loans, minister-at-large services, materials, and occasional leadership training. Districts were to pick up most of the follow-up services to new and not-so-new fellowships. The UUA Congregational Services department offered growth workshops for small congregations and resources to help district staff work with these congregations.

At the same time, the UUA decided to reduce the amount and length of its subsidy to congregations transitioning to church status. The earlier subsidy started at $3,000 the first year and was reduced by $300 a year over ten years. The policy adopted in the early 1960s started at $2,000, with annual reductions of $500 a year for a five-year period.

After 1967, district executives were the primary agents for initiating fellowships. The Extension Department simply provided guides and other materials and oversaw affiliation and recognition.

Since the end of the extension ministry program and its financial aid for transitions in 2004, the responsibility for supporting smaller congregations and helping at least some of them transition to full-time ministry has fallen even more heavily on the districts. District offices recruit people who can serve as part-time consulting ministers and make them available to congregations that are not yet large enough to afford a full-time minister. Districts enlist active or retired ministers (sometimes from other denominations), student ministers, and even skilled laypersons. Rev. Tom Chulak, the St. Lawrence district executive, reports that he has never failed to match a congregation with someone who can work with them, although sometimes that person is slow in appearing. The consulting minister's services include limited preaching, working with committees, and providing advice. Chulak believes that with such support, every small, struggling congregation has the potential to survive and grow.

Some district executives also now recommend that the first full-time minister be an interim minister. An interim minister is someone who serves on a temporary basis (usually for one or two years) and is specifically trained to help the congregation prepare for a more permanent minister. Although they are usually thought of as helping to transition between former and future settled ministers, their training makes them suited to this kind of transition as well. Interim ministers can help members overcome their resistance to authority and learn to share leadership. As a result, the first settled minister is less likely to struggle with these issues.

Providing financial support for a congregation's first settled minister is another challenge that now falls to the districts. Most districts have Chalice Lighter programs to solicit donations from individual members around the district. This money is used to fund ministers, buildings, and other financial needs of growing congregations.

The Church of the Larger Fellowship

Another important resource for surviving small fellowships, and small congregations in general, is the Church of the Larger Fellowship (CLF). This organization provides a wealth of resources—including print materials and a web site—for geographically isolated Unitarian Universalists. CLF serves not only individuals but also small groups, whether or not they are formally organized in a congregation. Groups of fewer than 50 people can enroll in the Church on Loan program, which offers worship, religious education, and adult study materials designed specifically for such groups. CLF also offers their monthly publication *Quest*, the *uu&me!* insert in *UU World* magazine, and an email list for small congregations. CLF is sometimes the nucleus for a new congregation that would have started as a largely unaided, unsupervised lay-led fellowship in earlier times. Thus, CLF does some of the work today that was done by the Fellowship Office between 1948 and 1967.

The transition from fellowship to church is inevitably accompanied by some pain. But in the end, it usually brings great satisfaction. After hundreds of such transitions since the beginning of the fellowship movement, the lessons of experience have taken root. The resources of the districts, the Congregational Services department, and the Church of the Larger Fellowship are helping to ease the transition for today's fledgling churches. Raising the size requirement for chartering new churches has also been a key strategy. It ensures that these limited but crucial resources will not be spent on long periods of nurturing very small groups, but are instead focused where they can make the most difference in growing healthy and vital congregations.

The Survivors

Forty years after the end of the fellowship movement, about 40 percent of the hundreds of little lay-led congregations planted from Cape Cod to Alaska and from Minnesota to the Virgin Islands survive in some form. Some are still small and lay-led. Others have evolved into full-service congregations with buildings, ministers, and religious education programs. Congregations in different regions of the country had different experiences, depending on the unique geographic, historical, and cultural contexts in which they emerged. This chapter provides an overview of the survivors and defines the five regions to be explored in subsequent chapters.

Determining how many congregations were founded as lay-led fellowships between 1948 and 1967 is not a simple task. The data provided here on congregations—including membership, ministered status, and date of founding—is from the 2005 (and sometimes 2004) directory of the Unitarian Universalist Association, supplemented by data from earlier directories where appropriate. The directories are vulnerable to occasional errors, most often of omission. They also do not document how a congregation began. It is not easy to determine whether a congregation began as a true lay-led fellowship rather than a spin-off sponsored by a nearby congregation or a denominationally financed new start. The main resource for the first ten years of the fellowship movement is Laile

Bartlett's *Bright Galaxy*, supplemented by field reports from Munroe Husbands. The rest of the information comes from the archival records of the Extension Department and the Fellowship Office, as well as histories of individual congregations gleaned from district compilations, interviews, web sites, and email correspondence.

Whether or not a congregation began as a lay-led fellowship is not always clear. In some cases, such as South Nassau in New York or Hamden in Connecticut, the lay-led fellowship period was so brief that it is nearly forgotten when recounting the congregation's history. I do not count as fellowships those congregations that began with ministers and were sponsored by the AUA or UUA, nor do I include spin-offs from established congregations. The line between spin-offs and lay-led fellowships was often hard to draw, so the numbers reported are educated and conservative guesses.

If birth records are difficult to verify, deaths are even harder. Congregations rarely die dramatic deaths; more often, they simply fade from the scene. In compiling statistics for the period from 1948 to 1958, Laile Bartlett lists 40 fellowships that did not survive. Munroe Husbands, in a 1962 pamphlet *Seven Life-preservers for Unitarian Universalist Fellowships*, claims that the mortality rate for fellowships organized in the first 14 years was about 10 percent.

In a memo from the same year, Husbands identified seven critical factors leading to the early demise of fellowships. Those that failed were usually formed with fewer than 15 members, had only a few dominant leaders, and met in members' homes rather than public places. They tended to have programs that were more like debating societies or study clubs than churches, and they usually offered no children's religious education program. Most also received limited financial commitments and remained isolated from other congregations and the district. An earlier memo by Husbands identified factors leading to the demise of three congregations. Bellingham, Washington, which lasted for eight months, was organized by a nearby minister who subsequently left the area; Bowling Green, Ohio, had mostly student members; and Lubbock, Texas, lost its best leaders early in the process.

Any count of the number of congregations that started, failed, and survived must be considered approximate. After piecing together information from various sources, a reasonable estimate suggests that out of 600 to 800 lay-led fellowships started between 1948 and 1967, 323 congregations survive. These survivors account for 30 percent of the UUA's present 1,060 congregations, with about 51,000 members out of the UUA's 159,000.

Some of these surviving congregations remain small for a variety of reasons. Some have resisted growth, while others are in small, isolated communities with little potential for growth. On the other hand, some first-wave fellowships have grown to more than 1,000 members. The membership levels of the survivors are as follows:

- 50 members or fewer: 71 congregations, average size of 27 members, aggregate membership of 2,000.
- 51 to 100 members: 70 congregations, average size of 70 members, aggregate membership of 5,000.
- More than 100 members: 186 congregations, average size of 237 members, aggregate membership of 44,000.

The average size of all surviving first-wave fellowships is about 150 members, the same as for all UUA congregations. Over 70 percent of these 323 congregations have at least part-time ministers. For the most part, then, the congregations that have survived to the present day are statistically similar to the UUA as a whole.

Although denominational support for fellowship development ended in 1967, the model lingers on. Many new congregations have been birthed in the 40 years since the end of the program. Most of them follow some variant of the fellowship creation story minus Munroe Husbands, often with the district providing the information and support needed to get the group up and running. The fellowship movement can take credit not just for the first-wave fellowships, but also for some of the new congregations started in the late 1960s and 1970s, when earlier visits and attempts finally bore fruit. Almost one UU member and one UU congregation in three is directly or indirectly a consequence of the fellowship movement.

The Five Regions

Fellowships are not formed in a vacuum, but in a context—cultural, historical, and geographic. Each region has its own story to tell, with both common features and unique developments. The next five chapters explore the congregations that arose from the fellowship movement in each of five regions. These chapters attempt to bring the movement to life by capturing some of the creation stories, the transition struggles, and the flavor of the fellowship experience as it was shaped by regional contexts.

Any regional division is somewhat arbitrary. West Virginia could be considered part of the South or the Midwest. Southerners always question whether Florida is really part of the South, and it is hard to find consensus about what constitutes the Midwest and the Southwest. The divisions presented here reflect in part some shared political, economic, cultural, and religious history within each region. Census divisions and UUA district lines were also factors in defining these five regions of approximately equal population:

- Northeast—11 states: Connecticut, Maine, Massachusetts, New Hampshire, Rhode Island, Vermont, Delaware, Maryland, New Jersey, New York, and Pennsylvania, plus the District of Columbia. UUA districts: Northeast, New Hampshire–Vermont, Massachusetts Bay, Ballou-Channing, Clara Barton, Metro New York, and St. Lawrence, plus parts of Joseph Priestley and Ohio-Meadville.
- Southeast—10 states: Virginia, North Carolina, South Carolina, Georgia, Florida, Alabama, Mississippi, Tennessee, Arkansas, and Louisiana. UUA districts: all of Thomas Jefferson, Mid-South, and Florida, plus parts of Joseph Priestley and Southwest.

- Midwest—14 states: West Virginia, Ohio, Kentucky, Indiana, Illinois, Michigan, Wisconsin, Minnesota, Iowa, Missouri, Kansas, Nebraska, and North and South Dakota. UUA districts: Heartland, Prairie Star, and Central Midwest, plus most of Ohio-Meadville.
- Southwest and Intermountain West—10 states: Montana, Idaho, Utah, Wyoming, Texas, Oklahoma, Colorado, Arizona, New Mexico, and Nevada. UUA districts: Mountain Desert plus parts of Southwest and Pacific Central.
- Pacific West—5 states: California, Oregon, Alaska, Washington, and Hawaii. UUA districts: parts of Pacific Northwest, Pacific Central, and Pacific Southwest.

Each of the five regions is home to approximately 20 percent of surviving first-wave fellowships. The next five chapters examine the diverse regional experience of the fellowship movement in those distinctly different geographic and cultural settings.

The Northeast

More than 40 percent of all Unitarian Universalists live in the Northeast region, consisting of New England, the Mid-Atlantic states, and the District of Columbia. During the fellowship period from 1948 to 1967, 65 fellowships were founded in this region. Today, the average size of surviving first-wave fellowships in the Northeast is just over 200 members, well above the average for other regions and for all UU congregations. Additional statistics about this region are provided in the table on page 120.

The most significant factor shaping the fellowship movement in the Northeast was the region's role as the birthplace of Unitarianism. As the fellowship program began, the Northeast was home to not only denominational headquarters in Boston, but also a large number of established churches, both Unitarian and Universalist. These churches gave rise to many spin-off congregations. Even fellowships that began independently could often count on support from other congregations to help them over the hurdles to growth.

But other factors also helped shape the first-wave fellowships in the Northeast. Compared to other regions, the Northeast had more urbanization, suburban development, and commerce. It had a greater concentration of colleges and universities, and its residents had, on average, higher levels of education and income. Fellowships in the Northeast drew a larger proportion of members from Catholicism and Judaism than in other regions, resulting in frequent controversies over the name "church" and the celebration of Christian holidays.

Since the end of the fellowship movement, the Northeast region has added just 42 new congregations—only about one a year. The high concentration of established Unitarian Universalist churches, together with slow population growth, has shifted the center of growth in Unitarian Universalism to the South and West.

Mid-Atlantic States

Most of the 65 first-wave fellowships in the Northeast region were concentrated in four Mid-Atlantic states: New York, Pennsylvania, Maryland, and New Jersey. Fellowships contributed significantly to the expansion of Unitarianism in the new and growing suburbs of the major cities of the Mid-Atlantic, particularly New York City, Philadelphia, and Washington, D.C.

Because Unitarianism was a familiar "brand" of religion in the region, fellowships in the area did not encounter as much cultural hostility. And because there was often a congregation or two nearby to provide support, many fellowships in this area avoided extreme forms of fellowship culture.

New York. The 17 surviving first-wave fellowships in New York include four in the immediate New York City area, five on Long Island, and eight in upstate communities. During the fellowship period, Long Island was booming as a suburb of New York City, and it had only two established congregations (Shelter Rock and Garden City). The fellowship movement added five more. This explains the relatively large number of fellowships planted on Long Island. The surviving Long Island fellowships are South Nassau, Huntington, Stony Brook, Bellport, and Muttontown. The Long Island congregations, both older and newer, have a history of mutual aid and support, coordinated through the Long Island Area Council.

The South Nassau congregation was organized in 1949 and called its first minister just a year later. That minister was Lon Ray Call himself, who had helped shape the fellowship movement. Call served that congregation for ten years, during which the congregation increased its membership and constructed a building.

Huntington called its first minister in 1962, after initially deadlocking in a 30–30 vote over the call. The controversy over whether to call a minister or remain lay-led was closely linked to the theist-humanist division, as it was in many lay-led fellowships. Fortunately for Huntington, the minister who stepped into this divisive situation was Ralph Stutzman, who was able to bring the congregation from "either-or" to "both-and" on many issues. He shared the pulpit with lay leaders and encouraged the coexistence of different theological orientations. From a rocky start, this congregation became a good model of shared ministry for other transitioning fellowships on Long Island.

Both Stony Brook, which had a university base (SUNY–Stony Brook), and Bellport, with membership grounded in Brookhaven National Laboratory, began with a strong humanist orientation. Stony Brook has, like Huntington, grown into a midsize, ministered congregation with a building and a religious education program. Bellport remained insistently lay-led and still has only about 60 members. The tiny congregation in Muttontown has failed to thrive despite help from other congregations in the area.

Of the upstate congregations, some benefited from older established congregations like the one in Buffalo. Four are scattered along the state's eastern border, from Plattsburg in the far north down to Glens Falls, Croton-on-Hudson, and Poughkeepsie. There had been a Unitarian church in Poughkeepsie from 1913 to 1932. Thus, the Poughkeepsie fellowship, organized in 1952, is one of the rare "revival stories" in the Northeast (they are more commonly found in the South and Midwest). The fellowships in Hamburg and Big Flats remain very small (less than 20 members). The rest of the surviving fellowships in upstate New York are in the small to midsize range, most served by ministers.

Delaware. The lone first-wave fellowship in Delaware was the Unitarian Universalist Fellowship of Newark. It began as an extension of the First Unitarian Church of Wilmington in 1955 and was incorporated as an independent group that October. The fellowship was lay-led from 1955 to 1969, served by a minister from 1969 to 1975, lay-led again from 1975 to 1985, and then obtained the services of an extension minister in 1986. Since that time the congregation has been served by full-time ministers. Their web site is a testimonial to the principle of shared ministry, stating that "we recognize the value of this professional leadership, while acknowledging and accepting the opportunities and responsibilities of an involved, supportive, and committed congregation." Newark today has nearly 200 members.

New Jersey. New Jersey's nine surviving first-wave fellowships are split between the Metro New York and Joseph Priestley districts. Three of the nine (Cherry Hill, Princeton, and Morristown) claim more than 250 members. At the other extreme are two lay-led fellowships with less than 50 members, Lakeland (23) and Skylands (49).

Surprisingly, there was no Unitarian congregation in Princeton prior to the fellowship movement. It would seem to have been an obvious location—in a densely populated urban state, home to an Ivy League university, sure to attract faculty as well as other religious liberals. The fellowship held its first service in 1949 with 50 adults in attendance. Just over four years later, the congregation had grown large enough to qualify for church status. Shortly thereafter, with the help of the standard subsidy from the American Unitarian Association, it called its first minister. By 1957, it had a building to house the growing congregation and the 140 children in religious education.

With such a quick transition to a full-time minister, a building, and a sizeable church school, Princeton's history bears few marks of its fellowship beginnings. Today Princeton is a congregation of 458 members with a sizeable professional staff, a healthy endowment, an active social justice program, and a strong Partner Church program, supporting a historic Unitarian church in Feheregyhaza, Hungary.

Pennsylvania. Pennsylvania hosted 15 first-wave fellowships, 11 in the Joseph Priestley District and four in the Ohio-Meadville District. The fellowship movement came to a state already blessed with a number of Unitarian and Universalist churches, most from the 19th century, of which 14 are still in existence. Meadville, in northwest Pennsylvania, was home to a Unitarian seminary (which later moved to Chicago to become Meadville-Lombard). So the state had a solid foundation on which to build new congregations.

The largest surviving fellowship is Mainline Unitarian Church in Devon, established with 34 members in 1958 and now claiming 690 members. Four other surviving first-wave fellowships have more than 200 members. Only one remains very small: Joseph Priestley Unitarian Universalist Fellowship in Lewisburg, with 28 members.

Maryland. Maryland benefited from the outreach of three established congregations—All Souls in Washington, D.C., and the churches in Baltimore and Annapolis—that supported the development of new congregations as spin-offs. In all, 14 lay-led fellowships were established in Maryland between 1948 and 1967. Some of them moved very quickly to become full-service, minister-led congregations. Others took longer. Hagerstown, for example, was established in 1957 and called its first full-time minister in 1999.

Towson began as a fellowship under the sponsorship of First Unitarian Church in Baltimore. It claims to be the fastest growing fellowship in Unitarian history, increasing its membership from 35 to 85 in just four months (from January to May 1960). By 1962 the Towson congregation had called a minister; ten years later it constructed its first building. Today it has 320 members.

Rockville began as an extension of the Unitarian Church of Montgomery County (now called the Cedar Lane Unitarian Universalist Church). Established in 1956, Rockville had a strong start, with 47 adults and 48 children at the first service. It only took four years for Rockville to "graduate" to church status, with 126 members and 148 children in religious education. Rockville now numbers over 300 members.

Maryland was also home to the last Universalist extension effort in the United States and the first church to include both Unitarian and Universalist in its name. Silver Spring was established as a lay-led Universalist fellowship in 1952. Like Towson and Rockville, it grew to a midsize congregation of 391 members.

New England

There was little need or motivation to plant lay-led fellowships in New England. For one thing, three of its six states—Maine, Massachusetts, and Rhode Island—lagged behind the rest of the country in population growth during the fellowship period. More significantly, the region was already home to hundreds of established Unitarian congregations. Massachusetts, the largest New England state, has a whopping 131 Unitarian churches that originated before the fellowship movement, all but three of which were established prior to 1900.

Connecticut was something of an exception to the New England pattern. It gained population during the period in question and had relatively few established Unitarian congregations (nine, just one more than tiny Rhode Island) because the Congregational church had maintained a firmer hold there than in Massachusetts. Five of the nine surviving first-wave fellowships in New England are in Connecticut. Of the surviving first-wave fellowships in New England, five remain small today (ranging from 13 to 45 members). The others have grown to sizeable, "full-service" congregations.

The Falmouth congregation on Cape Cod, organized in 1958, is the only first-wave fellowship organized in Massachusetts. The congregation was lay-led for 30 years, although it did have the benefit of clergy advice during that time. Ken Warren served as consulting minister for 20 years, followed by ten years of volunteer service from retired minister William Gardiner, a member of the congregation. After a successful experience with Arthur Wilmot, a minister-on-loan from Corvallis, Oregon, in 1988, Falmouth acquired an extension minister in 1989, who was then called as a settled minister in 1994.

The Unitarian Universalist Congregation of the Upper Valley, located in Norwich, Vermont, is a good example of a fellowship that went through many ups and downs before flourishing. Begun in the 1950s, this congregation actually owned their own building in the 1960s. But the civil rights movement and the Vietnam war divided the congregation. With a shrinking membership, the fellowship could no longer afford the building and disbanded in 1972. However, small groups kept the vision alive.

In 1984, 27 people started over, including some members from the earlier fellowship. Growth was slow but steady, with only two services a month in the early years. As in many congregations, a decisive event turned the tide. Nancy Jay Crumbine, a local college professor, decided to become a Unitarian Universalist minister. She was ordained in 1993 and became the congregation's first minister. A building finally became a reality in 1996. In 2001 Crumbine retired, and after two interim ministries, the congregation called Bruce Johnson in 2003. Today the congregation has 119 members and is actively engaged in a number of social justice issues. It takes particular pride in being a founding Green Sanctuary congregation and a strong supporter of civil unions for same-sex couples in Vermont.

Today

The Northeast was less impacted by the fellowship movement than other regions of the country because Unitarianism already had such a strong presence in the area. Even in this historically Unitarian region, however, the fellowship movement made significant contributions in expanding Unitarianism to the new and growing suburbs of major cities. While there are still small fellowships in this territory, a large proportion of the Northeast's first-wave fellowships grew quickly into medium-sized, ministered congregations—more, on average, than in any other region.

The Southeast

The Southeast region includes Virginia, North Carolina, South Carolina, Georgia, Florida, Alabama, Mississippi, Tennessee, Arkansas, and Louisiana. All of the Thomas Jefferson, Mid-South, and Florida districts lie within this region, along with parts of the Joseph Priestley and Southwest districts. Statistics about this region are provided in the table on page 121.

Unitarianism in the Southeast has experienced, for the most part, a lonely journey in a hostile culture. Yet the Southeast was a fertile field for the fellowship movement, which fueled a Unitarian revival in the region. Sixty-nine first-wave fellowships survive today, accounting for about one-quarter of all Unitarian Universalist membership in the region. Forty-four percent of current congregations in the Southeast trace their history to the fellowship movement.

Unitarianism had taken hold in this region much earlier. Prior to the Civil War, there were active Unitarian congregations in many Southern cities, including Mobile, Birmingham, Augusta, Savannah, Charleston, Richmond, Memphis, and New Orleans. One of the most famous sons of the South, John C. Calhoun of South Carolina, who served as Vice President under both Adams and Jackson, was a Unitarian. Although there was no Unitarian congregation in the lightly settled region of upstate South Carolina, he was a founding member of All Souls Church in Washington, D.C., in 1822. The Charleston church, which split from the Congregational church in the 1820s, was the mother church of many other Unitarian congregations in the region.

The Civil War and the hostilities leading up to it created an ever-widening breach between Unitarians in the North and those in the South. Only four Unitarian congregations in the South (outside of Florida) survived the Civil War: Richmond, Charleston, Memphis, and New Orleans.

Universalism fared somewhat better, continuing to thrive in the South after the war, at least for a time. In the late 1800s, Universalist missionary Quillen Shinn traveled throughout the rural South establishing lay-led Universalist house churches in small towns. But as the South became industrialized and people moved to the cities, one by one most of these little rural churches closed their doors. A few still survive—Canon and Winder in Georgia, Outlaw's Bridge and Red Hill in North Carolina, Clayton Memorial in South Carolina, and Camp Hill in Alabama.

Planting the Faith

The timing of the fellowship movement could not have been better suited to reaping a rich harvest in the Southeast. After World War II, an increasing number of people from other parts of the country moved to this region, for several reasons. The war introduced many servicemen and servicewomen to the South, which has a large number of military bases. Industry began moving to the South, especially from New England. The advent of air conditioning made the southern climate more livable.

During the 1950s and 1960s, the AUA funded a few new start clergy-led churches in urban areas of the Southeast, including Charlotte and Knoxville. In addition, some existing congregations supported the development of new congregations. The Asheville congregation, for example, sponsored several spin-offs in the immediate area. But the dominant story of Unitarianism, and later

Unitarian Universalism, in the Southeast during this time was the isolated, lay-led fellowship. Munroe Husbands made several trips to this region, establishing local congregations in Virginia, the Carolinas, Georgia, Florida, and Alabama. By 1958, when Laile Bartlett wrote her ten-year retrospective on the fellowship movement, 53 lay-led fellowships held regular services in these ten states. Most of these congregations have continued to the present day.

Even after the fellowship movement ended in 1967, lay-led congregations continued to spring up. The UUA directory lists 69 new congregations established in the region since 1967. Only a few of them were deliberate new starts by the UUA; the rest arose more or less spontaneously. Of these newer congregations, half remain lay-led today.

Southeastern congregations are most often located in either college towns or large metropolitan areas. College towns with first-wave fellowships include Charlottesville and Blacksburg in Virginia; Raleigh, Durham, and Chapel Hill in North Carolina; Clemson, South Carolina; Athens, Georgia; Tuscaloosa, Alabama; and Oxford, Mississippi. But the Southeast also has small, isolated congregations in rural areas, like the fellowship in Mountain Home, Arkansas. Despite seeing little hope for growth in what is largely a retirement community, it remains a Unitarian Universalist outpost in a remote part of the South. Mississippi, also a very rural state, has only six small congregations, none with a minister.

The Atlantic and Gulf coasts have been a major population growth area. Coastal cities in this region (outside Florida) boast 14 congregations, many of them relatively new.

Revivals

Revival is a popular term in southern religious culture. It usually refers to a series of emotional services in which sinners are called back into relationship with Jesus. Although this sort of revivalism is not a part of Unitarian Universalist culture, we do have our own revival stories. With the help of the fellowship movement, two congregations that had died out before the Civil War reemerged from the ashes.

The Mobile, Alabama, congregation, organized in 1836, was served briefly by noted 19th-century Unitarian minister James Freeman Clarke and subsequently by eight other Unitarian ministers between 1836 and 1851. By 1842, however, the Mobile congregation fell on hard times as the split between northern and southern Unitarians over the slavery issue took its toll. According to the congregation's own history, after 1849 there were still individual Unitarians in Mobile, but there was no church, society, or fellowship. It wasn't until the 1950s that organized Unitarianism returned to Mobile. In 1950, Rev. Robert Weston helped to organize the state's first fellowship in Fairhope, just across the bay from Mobile. The Fairhope group in turn encouraged Mobile to organize a lay-led fellowship. After several false starts, the fellowship was formally birthed in 1958 and completed a building in 1971. Although it has been served by several extension ministers and visiting ministers, it remains lay-led and small (35 members).

Savannah has a more dramatic and successful revival story. The Savannah congregation calls itself "the Jingle Bells Church" because the composer of that Christmas carol, James Pierpont, was the congregation's music director when he copyrighted the song in 1857. After the congregation folded in 1859, its church building in downtown Savannah was sold to the Episcopal diocese, which moved it to another section of town. There it served an African American Episcopal congregation until the 1940s. The building was then sold to a Baptist congregation. In the meantime, after two unsuccessful attempts in the early 1950s, the Unitarian congregation re-emerged as a lay-led fellowship in 1958. The congregation graduated first to part-time ministry and then, in 1991, to full-time ministry. Audrey Vincent, the first full-time minister (now retired), arranged for her installation to be held in the Baptist church, the historic home of the Unitarian congregation. Careful cultivation of a good relationship with the Baptists elicited a promise that the Unitarians would have the right of first refusal when the Baptist congregation was ready to sell. In the interim, the Unitarian congregation was meeting in a nearby historic house that was bursting at the seams.

In 1996, the Savannah congregation, now numbering over 100 members, was able to purchase and reoccupy its historic church building, although the reoccupation has been plagued by structural problems. Back in its historic space, the Savannah congregation represents a vital link between the early history of Unitarianism in the South and the expanding presence of Unitarian Universalism in the modern South.

The fellowship movement in the Southeast was unique. Certainly the break with the North that drove religious liberalism underground in the mid-19th century was an unusual circumstance. But a century later, three cultural issues surrounding the reestablishment of religious liberalism in the South are particularly significant: the civil rights movement, the dominant evangelical culture, and an influx of Unitarian Universalists and liberal Christians from the Northeast and Midwest.

The Civil Rights Movement

When Unitarian Universalists reflect on their role in the civil rights movement, they often turn to the stories of Viola Liuzzo and Rev. James Reeb, two northern UUs who became martyrs of the activism in Selma. In the 1960s, many Unitarian Universalists from the North carried on the proud history of their abolitionist forebears by going to the South to participate in demonstrations and marches in support of civil rights. But the untold story is the resident white southern Unitarian Universalists who, when the marches were over and the outside supporters went home, continued to fight the good fight among their neighbors and coworkers. Many congregations in the Southeast were active in the civil rights movement, a stance that alienated many of their white fellow citizens, while not attracting African Americans to the movement in any great numbers.

The stories of two of those congregations, both in Alabama, deserve special attention. The Birmingham fellowship was established in 1954 in a community that had two previous Unitarian congregations, one prior to the Civil War and one in the 1920s. During the 1960s, the Birmingham fellowship frequently hosted demonstrators, marchers, and civil rights workers from other states. The congregation was the target of hate messages and bomb threats. One member of the Birmingham congregation told the story of the church secretary who responded wearily to yet another bomb threat with "Take a number!"

Tuscaloosa's fledgling fellowship fell victim to the controversy over civil rights and took decades to recover. The congregation had an impressive 120 members when Autherine Lucy made the first attempt to integrate the University of Alabama. No congregation, black or white, would invite her to worship—except the Unitarian fellowship in Tuscaloosa. Overnight, their membership dropped from 120 to 11. At one point in the tenacious fellowship's history, only six members remained. Today there is a thriving congregation in Tuscaloosa with nearly 100 members, a building, a minister, and proud memories of standing up for civil rights at great cost.

While the Tuscaloosa story is dramatic, it is not unique. Laile Bartlett records similar pressures on the Jacksonville, Florida, fellowship, organized in 1950. It had difficulty finding a meeting place because its meetings were integrated in a racially segregated community. Conflicts over segregation led the members to conclude that only ownership of a building would make it possible for them to continue to exist. They found property in a residential community. But the local authorities declared the fellowship ineligible to build there because the area was zoned for houses and churches only, and a fellowship was not a church. Fortunately, the fellowship had the required number of members to qualify as a church. After the American Unitarian Association hastily processed the application for church status, the congregation was able to occupy the property.

Evangelical Culture

Unitarian Universalist congregations in most regions of the country claim to be a beleaguered beacon of religious liberalism surrounded by fundamentalists and evangelicals who regard them as hell-bound, irreligious, or a dangerous influence. Nowhere is this more true than in the Southeast, where conservative and evangelical Christianity is very strong. One young mother who moved to the South told the story of being badgered about where she went to church; she was repeatedly urged to bring her child to Sunday school or Bible school. Finally, she said in exasperation, "Oh, didn't I tell you? I'm home-churching!"

Unitarian Universalist congregations welcome those who, feeling similarly pressured to have a church identity, find this liberal faith the most acceptable option. Until recently, those new to Unitarian Universalism in the Southeast have mainly been refugees from the conservative wing of Christianity—Southern Baptist, Wesleyan Methodist, Pentecostal. More recently, Unitarian Universalist congregations have experienced a large influx of the unchurched. Only in the last few decades could one claim unchurched status in the Southeast without being something of a pariah.

Lay-led fellowships often provide a refuge for those who consider themselves victims of religious abuse. But without ministerial leadership, they offer no good way to "unpack the baggage" from such negative experiences. Anticlerical attitudes can become strongly entrenched as a result. Visitors with a liberal Christian background were often surprised to encounter a religious community in which "bashing" Christianity was commonplace and accepted.

While Unitarianism, and later Unitarian Universalism, has encountered rejection everywhere, that rejection has been particularly intense in the Southeast. In many religiously conservative Southern communities, Unitarians have been excluded from the larger life of the community. Unitarian fellowships—with their seemingly strange folkways, lack of ministerial leadership, and refusal to proclaim themselves part of the Christian mainstream—are often not welcome at the interfaith table in many such communities. Interfaith gatherings are more often labeled ecumenical—meaning Christian unity rather than a broader inclusiveness. Fellowships wanting to participate in community ministries are frequently left out. Unitarian Universalist youth have encountered misunderstanding, concern, or hostility from teachers and fellow students, including threats of going to hell. (Catholics in the South report similar experiences, especially outside urban areas.) This isolation from the larger faith community has often created a fortress mentality that is at odds with Unitarian Universalism's commitment to diversity, openness, and respect for the inherent worth and dignity of every person.

New Arrivals

Unitarian lay-led fellowships throughout the country have found that a significant part of their membership consists of those who came to the region from elsewhere. In the Southeast, newcomers have been particularly important in starting or growing lay-led fellowships.

Many of these newcomers have been college faculty. In the 1950s and 1960s, small parochial Southern colleges were jolted into growth, first by the GI Bill and later by the arrival of baby boomers. Searching for qualified faculty, the colleges recruited from outside the region. They often hired graduates of doctoral programs of larger, established universities in the Northeast and Midwest. Historically, but particularly in the 1960s, college faculty have been more politically and religiously liberal than society as a whole. Certainly they tend to be more intellectual in their approach to many aspects of life, including religion. Some faculty members coming from outside the Southeast were already Unitarians or Unitarian Universalists. Others quickly found a hospitable religious home, and sometimes a venue for self-expression, in lay-led fellowships.

In more metropolitan areas, newcomers arrived as manufacturing companies moved from the Northeast and the Midwest to the South in search of cheap labor and land, mild climate, abundant water resources, and a pro-business political environment. For some of these newcomers, Unitarianism or Unitarian Universalism was not their native religious tongue. But it bore a closer resemblance to the liberal Christian churches back home than the local, more conservative Methodist, Baptist, or Presbyterian churches. That was the case for a number of people who came to Greenville, South Carolina, in the 1950s and 1960s. After scoping out the local church scene, they took refuge in the Unitarian fellowship as a more familiar kind of religious environment. Some of these newcomers brought with them the knowledge of "how to do church." They knew about worship, outreach, religious education, finance, and the role of a minister. They knew how to orient and integrate new members and offer pastoral care. They helped an intellectual religious club transform itself into a religious community.

Florida

With only four Unitarian churches prior to 1948, Florida was ripe territory for the development of lay-led fellowships in the 1950s and 1960s. The state has also benefited from the intentional planting of new minister-led congregations by the AUA and UUA over the years. Today Florida has 43 congregations and a total membership of 5,154, about one-fourth of all Unitarian Universalists in the ten Southern states. Seventeen of those congregations are products of the fellowship movement.

At least one of those fellowships qualifies as a revival: Tampa, which grew out of a Great Books discussion group in the 1950s. This fellowship's predecessor was a short-lived effort by the American Unitarian Association to establish a ministered congregation in Tampa between 1930 and 1934. Rumors of violent conflict with the Ku Klux Klan surrounded its demise in the 1930s. Conflict with the larger community was also a problem for the later fellowship, this time over its biracial makeup.

Northern Florida, from the panhandle down to the Ocala area, is very similar in history and culture to its neighbors to the north,

Georgia and Alabama. All of this area, and most of the interior of Florida north of the Everglades, was heavily agricultural during the fellowship period. Orlando was a relatively undeveloped area when Disney World began to be built nearby in the late 1960s.

But sunny coastal Florida, from St. Augustine on the Atlantic coast and Clearwater on the Gulf down to the southern tip, was a different story. In the last half of the 20th century, this area had a huge influx of newcomers—heavily, but not entirely, retirees. Natives were scarce. Everyone seemed to be from somewhere else, many with deep roots back in New England or the Midwest that often included a liberal religious heritage. Many retirees wanted a Unitarian congregation only during the winter months, because they returned north as summer approached. Such part-year residents, or "snowbirds," are common in Florida and have created a state of transients. Under these circumstances, it has been challenging to build community within a congregation, let alone develop support between congregations.

Some aspects of fellowship culture have been especially strong in Florida. Retirees are often resistant to change and uninterested in developing religious education programs. Those who are native to Unitarianism or Unitarian Universalism are of an age group likely to have been shaped by flat-earth humanism. On the other hand, those who come from more traditional northern Unitarian churches tend to be less resistant to obtaining buildings and ministers as their fellowships grow.

Today

Unitarian Universalist growth in the Southeast continues apace after the end of the fellowship period. The southeastern states still gain population at a rate greater than the national average, although more and more of the newcomers are retirees seeking cheaper living costs and a milder climate. In parts of the region, especially Florida, Unitarian Universalist congregations have many gray heads and empty religious education classrooms.

Lay-led congregations continue to spring up. The Florida and Thomas Jefferson districts have among the highest rates of new congregation formation of all UU districts in the country. The 2005 UUA directory lists 74 congregations that were established between 1968 and 2004 in the Southeast, 36 of which are still lay-led. Many of these newer lay-led congregations need services and support (especially part-time and consulting ministry) as they struggle to transition into full-fledged congregations with clergy, religious education programs, and buildings of their own. District executives in the Thomas Jefferson, Mid-South and Florida districts report that their greatest challenge is meeting that demand.

The Midwest

The Midwest region consists of 14 states. Seven of them—West Virginia, Kentucky, Ohio, Michigan, Indiana, Illinois, and Wisconsin—are east of the Mississippi River. West of the Mississippi, the region includes Missouri, Kansas, Iowa, Nebraska, Minnesota, and North and South Dakota. These states make up most of the Ohio-Meadville district and all of the Heartland, Central Midwest, and Prairie Star districts. Statistics about this region are provided in the table on page 122.

The Midwest region is second only to the Northeast in its long historical tradition and rich diversity of Unitarian Universalist congregations. The region had 56 established churches in existence in 1948 that are still active today—more than any other region except the Northeast.

Ohio had a particularly strong Universalist presence (80 congregations) in the 19th century. A Unitarian presence in Kansas dates from a pre–Civil War struggle (known as "Bleeding Kansas") over whether the territory would be admitted to the Union as a slave state or a free state. Abolitionists from the East who came to take part in the struggle brought their Unitarianism with them and established several congregations, although only the one in Wichita remains today. In the 1880s Unitarian minister Jenkins Lloyd Jones, founder of All Souls Unitarian Church in Chicago, helped to establish a Norwegian Unitarian mission in Minnesota, an area where Universalism also took hold and spawned many congregations.

In the Midwest, then, liberal religion was not an oddity. This was particularly true in Illinois and Ohio, but also to a lesser extent in Michigan, Minnesota, Indiana, Iowa, and Wisconsin. With so many existing congregations, the fellowship movement had somewhat less impact here than in other regions; there was simply less need for it. At the same time, however, there was a much stronger foundation on which to extend Unitarianism than in other regions, especially the Southeast and the Intermountain West. Today the Midwest has 186 congregations and 36,000 members, as well as one of only two Unitarian Universalist seminaries, Meadville-Lombard Theological School at the University of Chicago.

Several factors help explain the relatively large number of pre-1948 congregations in the Midwest. One is the urban character of the region clustered around the Great Lakes. But any analysis of liberal religion in the Midwest would be incomplete without examining the many historical events and movements that left a lasting legacy of Unitarian Universalism in this large and diverse region.

The Iowa Sisterhood

Cynthia Grant Tucker's *Prophetic Sisterhood* chronicles the story of the Iowa Sisterhood, an energetic and diverse group of women ministers in the late 19th and early 20th centuries. These women, who included both Unitarian and Universalist ministers, were responsible for organizing 18 Unitarian societies in the Dakotas, Nebraska, Iowa, Michigan, Wisconsin, Illinois, and Minnesota.

The churches founded by the women of the Iowa Sisterhood were in many ways a precursor to the fellowship movement. They were not lay-led, since the women who served them were ordained, however reluctantly, by their Unitarian or Universalist faith traditions. But these congregations were started in much the same fashion as lay-led fellowships, and the Unitarian women ministers met the same kind of misgivings in Boston as did the fellowships more than a half-century later.

Women in ministry were widely considered to be an inferior substitute for male clergy. The women of the Iowa Sisterhood generally approached ministry differently from their male counterparts, with less emphasis on the intellectual Sunday sermon and more focus on pastoral care and social ministry within the community. These women clergy were also more egalitarian and more open to experimentation. In that respect, their churches reflected a frontier culture that was less anchored to tradition than congregations in the Northeast—again foreshadowing the fellowship movement. By the outbreak of World War I, however, the women ministers in these successful "start-from-scratch" congregations had all been replaced by male clergy.

Humanism and Prairie Populism

Humanism was a dominant theological perspective in many early lay-led fellowships, but especially in this region. The upper Midwest was particularly ripe for such congregations because it was the birthplace of the American Humanist Association. The area was home to Humanist leaders John Dietrich and Curtis Reese, both signers of the 1933 Humanist Manifesto.

As a theology centered on the meaning and purpose of human life, humanism was a natural bedfellow of political movements that tried to improve the welfare of the average person. Thus humanism found a kindred spirit in the Midwestern cultural phenomenon known as "prairie populism." This movement championed workers, farmers, and the poor. William Jennings Bryan, three-time Democratic candidate for president in the 1890s and early 1900s, was a prairie populist from Nebraska. He was best known for his "cross of gold" speech decrying the effects of the gold standard on the farmer and the working man ("you shall not crucify mankind upon a cross of gold"). In Wisconsin, Robert LaFollette's progressive policies as a member of Congress, a political reformer, and a journalist in the first few decades of the 20th century left a legacy of liberal politics that still pervades the region. Hubert Humphrey and Eugene McCarthy were products of Minnesota's brand of prairie populism and liberal politics. Senator Gaylord Nelson of Wisconsin is fondly remembered as the father of Earth Day in 1970. This faith in humankind's capacity to create heaven on earth resonates with the Unitarian Universalist commitment to social justice and the social gospel. Such a liberal, optimistic, egalitarian, this-worldly, socially concerned political and cultural environment was exceptionally hospitable to the fellowship movement.

The Fellowship Years

The fellowship movement came in the heyday of the industrial Midwest. The eastern part of this region was the industrial heartland of the nation, with major cities such as Detroit, Chicago, Indianapolis, Cleveland, and Cincinnati. Kentucky and West Virginia were more rural, but both had strong ties, in terms of employment and the ebb and flow of population, across the river to Ohio. Blue-collar workers were a significant part of the population, and many African Americans came from the South in the postwar years.

Throughout the region, major public universities emerged and grew to mega size. They included Ohio State, the University of Michigan, Michigan State, the University of Illinois, the University of Wisconsin, and Purdue. Together with the industries that brought scientists and engineers to the region, these universities provided a pool from which developing fellowships drew the humanist, rational, educated leaders that created their organizations, planned their buildings, and invented their own concepts of a Sunday service or program.

The fellowship movement supplemented established urban Unitarian and rural Universalist churches with a healthy scattering of fellowships. The Midwest is home to 68 surviving first-wave fellowships with a total membership of just over 9,000, about a quarter of the total membership in this region. Eleven of the congregations are in Illinois, eight each in Ohio and Wisconsin, and six each in Michigan and Indiana, with the other 27 scattered among the remaining nine states. The average first-wave congregation in the Midwest has about 138 members, slightly below average size.

Fellowships in this region were particularly likely to develop around universities or other clusters of professionals, such as the Menninger Foundation in Topeka. All of West Virginia's first-wave fellowships and most of Ohio's were either in small college communities or grounded in groups of scientists working for large industrial firms. These fellowships attracted faculty and professionals from the natural and social sciences. Under the influence of the humanist movement, they developed typical fellowship-style Sunday morning gatherings that were heavy on intellectual content and light on ritual, music, and other dimensions of worship.

In the Midwest, those who left other religions to come to Unitarian fellowships tended to have Methodist, Baptist, or sometimes Catholic backgrounds. Lay-led fellowships also attracted many Unitarians who had moved to the Midwest from other regions. More recently, as in most of the country, they have attracted people with no church background at all.

In part because of the large number of established churches in this region, it was not uncommon for fellowships to spin off from nearby established congregations, or at least receive support from them. Some of these established churches were sources of aid, members, and advice; others were just kindred souls and a nearby presence. The Lexington, Kentucky, fellowship got its start with help from Rev. Robert Weston from the Louisville congregation. In its first six years, Burlington, Iowa, was assisted by 27 successive Unitarian guest preachers, most of them from area congregations. White Bear Unitarian Church in Minnesota was a spin-off of St. Paul's Unity Unitarian Church. The Carbondale, Illinois, fellowship's long period of lay-led growth was in part due to the rich resources of the region in providing Sunday worship leaders. Ames, Iowa, the third fellowship created in the movement, began as a discussion group led by the minister from Des Moines—none other than Grant Butler, who subsequently worked with Munroe Husbands and served as minister-at-large at the AUA. An established Universalist church in Waterloo, Iowa, merged with the Cedar Falls Unitarian Fellowship in 1962.

Creation and Transition Stories

Individual fellowships developed in their own unique ways. However, the stories of some of them represent certain characteristics and trends common to groups of fellowships. The following four stories illustrate three kinds of growth trends in the region: revivals of previous congregations, rapid transitions from fellowships to churches, and slower transitions from fellowships to churches.

Topeka, Kansas. This fellowship was established in the early 1960s. An earlier Unitarian church in Topeka, dating from the 19th century, had merged with the local Congregational church during the latter part of the Depression. Topeka still has an elderly member or two who remembers the earlier Unitarian church, and the fellowship has retrieved some of its original stained glass windows as a link to its past.

Manhattan, Kansas. This was another first-wave fellowship that had been home to a Unitarian church that closed its doors during the Depression. There was only about a 20-year gap between the old church and the new-born fellowship.

Bloomington, Indiana. The fellowship in Bloomington could serve as a model for transitioning from fellowship to church with relatively few bumps. The fellowship organized in 1953. After Munroe Husbands chose the fellowship to be the first beneficiary of the minister-at-large program, Grant Butler and his wife Calla spent a productive three months in Bloomington in 1957. During that time, membership increased from 73 to 129. In 1958, the congregation voted to become a church and called its first minister. Today it has 365 members, an extensive staff, and an active social justice program.

Charleston, West Virginia. A much slower growth story comes from this congregation, founded in 1953. It was dominated by scientists and engineers who stayed in leadership roles for several decades. In the 1970s and 80s, these leaders struggled with the emerging trend toward greater spiritual expression. Like many congregations in smaller communities, Charleston hid its light under a bushel—specifically, in a building with no sign that looked like just another home in a residential neighborhood of small dwellings and narrow streets. In addition to being nearly invisible, this congregation was very slow to come to grips with the need for professional ministry. Finally, in 1988, an extension minister helped them over the hump. Today they enjoy the leadership of co-ministers, their sixth and seventh ministers in the last 18 years. With the help of ministerial leadership, Charleston eventually emerged from hiding into a building that is more visible and more centrally located, and had 114 members in 2006.

Today

As heavy industry has given way to high-tech and service industries, growth in the Midwest has slowed, and with it, expansion of congregations in many denominations. Still, 56 new Unitarian Universalist congregations have arisen in the region in the last 40 years. In the land of the Iowa Sisterhood, the prairie populists, Abraham Lincoln and William Jennings Bryan, Adlai Stevenson and Robert LaFollette, Frank Lloyd Wright and Jenkins Lloyd Jones, Unitarian Universalist congregations remain a lively religious presence. They are a beacon of liberal religion in a religiously conservative culture, and a bastion into which Unitarian Universalism can welcome refugees and pass the torch to the next generation of leadership.

The Southwest and Intermountain West

The Southwest and Intermountain West region covers a lot of territory—from Oklahoma, Texas, New Mexico, and Arizona at the southern end, up through the mountains and deserts of Nevada, Utah, Colorado, Wyoming, Idaho, and Montana in the north. Most of this region is in the Mountain Desert and Southwest districts, except for Nevada, which is part of the Pacific Southwest, and Idaho, which is in the Pacific Northwest. Despite a shared history of pioneers and frontier settlements, small towns and large ranches, empty spaces and national parks, a region this large encompasses great diversity. The Western traditions of independence and self-reliance mesh well with the characteristics of fellowship culture. Frontier culture is a way of life that shapes the character of Unitarian Universalism in a region far from Boston.

The ten states in this region are for the most part lightly populated. In fact, the entire region contains only 15 percent of the U.S. population. The fellowship model was ideally suited to such a situation, which may explain the large number of very early first-wave fellowships in this region. Six surviving fellowships date from 1948 or 1949: Phoenix and Tucson, Arizona; Boulder, Colorado (now located in Lafayette); Stillwater, Oklahoma; Albuquerque, New Mexico; and Beaumont, Brownsville, Amarillo, and Denton, Texas. Utah is the only state in the region that was not part of the fellowship movement. Additional statistics about this region are provided in the table on page 123.

Though sparsely populated in general, this region does have its urban centers. They include Dallas/Forth Worth, Houston, San Antonio, Oklahoma City, Tulsa, Denver/Boulder, Phoenix, Salt Lake City, Las Vegas, Albuquerque, and Santa Fe. Ten of the region's larger cities had an existing Unitarian congregation prior to the fellowship movement. Most of the urban areas generated at least one lay-led fellowship between 1948 and 1967, often several, even when there was an established church in the city. Had these cities been farther east, more of them might have been chosen as sites for Boston's limited plantings of financially supported minister-led churches.

Several of the early fellowships became large congregations. But with few established churches available for support, vast distances between towns, and a limited number of major population centers, many of the fellowships in this region have remained small and isolated. The average size of surviving first-wave fellowships is 125 members, the smallest of any region. Forty-six congregations in the region currently have less than 50 members. Without other Unitarian Universalist congregations nearby, it is difficult for these isolated fellowships to support one another or to find visiting ministers to lead worship. Participating in district meetings is also challenging, particularly in the Mountain Desert district, which stretches from Canada to Mexico. One exception to the problem of isolation has been in the Denver area. There, small congregations have found that Iliff, a liberal Christian seminary in Denver with a number of Unitarian Universalist seminarians, is a useful source of student ministers and consulting ministers.

From 1940 to 1970, a time span that bracketed the fellowship movement, the U.S. population nearly doubled. A few states in this region (Oklahoma, Montana, Idaho, and Wyoming) lagged behind in this growth. The others, however, grew faster than the national average—especially Arizona and Nevada, states that attracted retirees. Nevada's population grew from only 77,000 in 1940 to almost half a million in 1970, while Arizona's grew from 334,000 to 1.8 million in the same time period.

Newcomers from other parts of the country brought their ethnic, religious, and cultural backgrounds with them. Some came from a Unitarian or Unitarian Universalist background and sought out such a congregation. Most of the Southwest and Intermountain West congregations interviewed for this book reported that their members include a fairly balanced mix of natives and newcomers to the region. Since the end of the fellowship movement, another 49 new congregations have been organized in the region, including 19 in Texas alone, partly as a result of population growth. Many of these new congregations have been lay-led, at least initially.

Most of the states in this region have relatively high Native American and Hispanic populations. However, for the most part, Unitarian Universalist congregations have not attracted many people from these groups.

A few states in this region have a distinctive cultural flavor because of the dominance of the Mormon church. In some areas, ex-Mormons are a significant source of new members in Unitarian Universalist congregations. Other congregations in the region draw from the more typical groups: newcomers, the unchurched, and refugees from conservative Christian traditions.

Creation and Transition Stories

Many of the fellowships in this region have followed a path similar to fellowships in other parts of the country. But this region also offers a diversity of fellowship stories informed by the wide open spaces and the tradition of western independence.

Greeley, Colorado. Universalist Horace Greeley encouraged a group of pioneers to move west in 1870, where they established a town in Colorado named for him. A Unitarian society was organized in Greeley in 1880; it later became the Unity Unitarian Church and in 1908 called a minister. This congregation disbanded in 1926, selling its building and disbursing its last assets in 1938. Just 23 years later, in 1961, Unitarian Universalism returned to Greeley in the form of a newly created fellowship. In 1967 the president of the UUA, Dana McLean Greeley (a cousin of Horace), visited the fellowship. Since then the congregation has had numerous ups and downs, with various meeting sites and intermittent or part-time service by professional ministers. When we visited with members of the Greeley congregation in 2004, after they had sold their building and ended their contract with a part-time minister, the congregation was frustrated and discouraged, meeting in an out-of-the way storefront church shared with another congregation. But at this writing, the fellowship—still without professional ministry—has once again found a building of its own.

Stillwater, Oklahoma. The Stillwater congregation is a lively outpost of liberal religion in a conservative college town, home of Oklahoma State University. Like many land-grant colleges, Oklahoma State puts more emphasis on scientific and technical disciplines than on the humanities and liberal arts. Humanists among the science and engineering faculty have always played a leadership role in Stillwater.

In 1946—even before the fellowship movement officially began—a group of religious liberals gathered in Stillwater to decide how to create a congregation of their own. Except for a lumber company owner, all the initial members were Oklahoma State faculty or their spouses. When the fellowship program officially began in 1948, Stillwater wanted to be the first fellowship recognized by the AUA, but the Boulder congregation beat them to the punch by just a few days.

The fledgling fellowship met on campus in the 1950s. Before long it organized a church school, which quickly grew to 19 children. In 1959, the congregation acquired its first building, a two-story house. A new church building, designed by an OSU faculty member from Transylvania, was constructed beginning in 1967 on land donated by a member. A dispute over lighting fixtures created a division between "slanters" and "levelers," but the congregation survived this episode of fellowship democracy to complete and occupy the building in the fall of 1969.

Ministers from the Unitarian churches in Tulsa and Oklahoma City periodically conducted services at Stillwater, usually in the evening so that they could be in their own pulpits on Sunday morning. In 1976, founding member and retired psychology professor Harry Brobst became the congregation's first full-time minister after returning to school to obtain a divinity degree. Brobst served until he retired in 1980. At that point, Stillwater was the only surviving fellowship from the small number founded in the 1940s that was without a minister. After several short stints of professional ministry, Stillwater decided in 1984 to share an extension minister with the Norman congregation, an arrangement that lasted not quite three years. Finally in 1988 Stillwater called Carol Fincher as a full-time minister, completing a second and this time more lasting transition to a minister-led congregation with a full range of congregational programs and services.

Stillwater today is a congregation of 78 members served by a minister, and is still in its church home from the 1960s. Like many other fellowships, it has survived its share of controversies—over social action; the role of professional ministry; and the change of its name, adding *Unitarian Universalist* and changing *fellowship* to *church*.

Reno, Nevada. The Reno congregation began as a lay-led fellowship in 1959. Its geographic isolation from other Unitarian Universalist congregations is fairly typical of the Intermountain West. After experimenting with part-time and extension ministry, the Reno congregation finally called its first full-time minister in 2003.

Durango, Colorado. The fellowship in Durango, a community isolated on the western slope of the Rockies, was established in 1967. With only 44 members, the congregation is not currently considering a professional minister. However, they have acquired a building and are working to expand their religious education offerings as a way of attracting new members.

Cheyenne, Wyoming. Established in 1961, this fellowship called co-ministers Robert and Makannah Morris in 1998 and has experienced considerable growth since then. The Morrises retired in 2006. Recently the congregation purchased a "used" church building from the Latter-day Saints, which fits their needs well. It may take some time to grow into, however—especially the indoor basketball court!

Dallas, Texas. The Oak Cliff fellowship in south Dallas was founded in 1961 on the very day that the Unitarians and Universalists merged, and thus holds the first charter issued by the Unitarian Universalist Association. The fellowship was organized as a spin-off of the First Unitarian Church of Dallas by members who wanted a shorter drive as well as the small size, loose organization, and freedom of a fellowship. Oak Cliff attributes its survival in part to the initial support and mentoring from First Church.

Oak Cliff was fortunate to have two successive extension ministers beginning in 1977, William Holway and Robert Hill. After Hill resigned to become the district executive in 1980, for a time the fellowship shared a minister with congregations in Denton and Arlington. Today the congregation, now called the Unitarian Universalist Church of Oak Cliff, is in a transitional state, with 60 members and leadership from a lay minister. Central to its identity is a strong pagan membership and pride in its attractive grounds, which include a labyrinth. They hope to grow in size to again be able to support full-time professional ministry.

Denton, Texas. The Denton fellowship, just north of Dallas, began with people meeting in homes in 1947 and was chartered in 1949. At first the group struggled with an identity that was more political (Democratic) and philosophical (humanist) than religious. A succession of ministers, as well as emerging lay leaders, helped the congregation transition to more typically Unitarian Universalist worship services. Religious education has always been an emphasis for this small congregation, which currently has 93 members. The Denton fellowship has struggled with finances, cultural clashes, resistance to growth, and the ups and downs of sharing ministers with other congregations, but continues to be a lively liberal religious presence on the north side of Dallas.

Albuquerque, New Mexico. A meeting of 30 interested people in May 1949 gave birth to the first lay-led fellowship in New Mexico. The group of 19 people who signed the charter began meeting at Temple Albert, the home of a Jewish congregation. When the temple was sold, the fellowship struggled. But by 1952 it was strong enough to call a minister, Franklin Smith, who arrived in January 1953. With 60 members, the fellowship became the First Unitarian Church of Albuquerque and established a church school. Today it is a congregation of 613 members in downtown Albuquerque, with three ministers, two professional religious educators, a music director, and a full-time administrator.

Phoenix, Arizona. Founded in 1947 (according to the congregation) or 1946 (according to the UUA directory), the Phoenix fellowship was lay-led until calling its first minister in 1957. It has now been served by ten ministers. The congregation currently meets in a building designed by a student of Frank Lloyd Wright and has a membership of 275.

Today

The Mountain Desert and Southwest district executives agree on their biggest challenge: helping lay-led fellowships, both old and new, transition to minister-led congregations with full programs and active participation in the larger movement. The extension program has served a number of congregations in the region, with largely positive results. However, some of the other strategies typically used to support fellowships are not well suited to this region. Shared ministers have been used in some areas where the distances are not too great, but the results have been mixed. Mutual support is often hard to come by; most of the opportunities are in the southern part of the region, where there are more congregations. The congregations to the north and west remain, for the most part, small and isolated. The current influx of population into some of these areas may help these congregations reach the critical size needed to provide the kind of worship, religious education, and community outreach programs that newcomers expect from a Unitarian Universalist congregation.

The Pacific West

All five of the Pacific states—California, Oregon, Washington, Alaska, and Hawaii—share not only an ocean but also a considerable distance from Boston. The Pacific West plays a particularly important part in the fellowship story, having the highest percentage of current congregations that were birthed during the fellowship movement. It is home to 69 surviving first-wave fellowships, 42 of them in California. The region straddles three districts of the Unitarian Universalist Association: Pacific Northwest, Pacific Central, and Pacific Southwest. Additional statistics about this region are provided in the table on page 124.

More than any other states, California, Oregon, Washington, and Alaska have been shaped by their pioneer history. Perhaps the region's spirit of independence and self-sufficiency accounts for its low percentage of church membership, well below the U.S. average. But that pioneer spirit resonates with the Unitarian emphasis on freedom, reason, tolerance, and respect for the individual, as well as with the do-it-yourself approach to religion that characterized the fellowship movement.

Urban centers in the three West Coast states are home to some long-established Unitarian Universalist congregations, including 15 in California. But rapid migration of population to the Pacific Coast in the period after World War II created a growth opportunity for religious communities, an opportunity quickly seized upon by the fellowship movement. While the U.S. population increased by more than 50 percent between 1940 and 1970, the West Coast states saw much more dramatic increases. Oregon and Washington doubled their populations during these three decades, while California's population rose from 3.4 million to just under 20 million.

The Pacific Northwest

The UUA's Pacific Northwest district—which includes Oregon, Washington, and Alaska (plus a large part of Idaho, covered in the previous chapter)—has a rich history of fellowship development. Spin-offs were significant in more urban areas of the district. The Seattle congregation assumed the role of developing new congregations, spinning off four in the area. However, most new congregations followed the traditional fellowship creation story.

By 1965, as the fellowship movement wound down, the district had 21 fellowships and only 11 churches. For several years during the 1960s, well-known writer Rev. Robert Fulghum served the district as fellowship consultant prior to becoming district executive. He was active in visiting and supporting the district's fellowships, including one trip in 1963 to the five congregations in Alaska.

Both Lon Ray Call and Munroe Husbands had close ties to the Pacific Northwest district. Call served several congregations in the district in his capacity as minister-at-large. He met and married his second wife while serving the Spokane congregation in 1943; helped establish congregations in Bellevue, Tacoma, and Bremerton, Washington; and served a year as interim minister in Bellevue in 1966–67. Munroe Husbands was a native of Spokane. As fellowship director, he made several trips to spark fellowships in the Pacific Northwest.

Anchorage, Alaska, was one of several congregations that sprang up in the wake of a visit from Munroe Husbands in 1955.

During its first seven years, the fellowship had seven meeting places, including two different elementary schools and a former nightclub. In 1963, the fellowship bought a building from the Assembly of God, a log cabin church that was dedicated by UUA president Dana Greeley that year. In 1969 the congregation, like many other lay-led fellowships, enjoyed the services of a minister-at-large for three months, leading to the call of its first full-time minister in 1970. Of the six congregations in Alaska, all of which started as lay-led fellowships (four between 1948 and 1967), Anchorage is the only one to have 35 years of history as a ministered congregation. The support of the denomination—Munroe Husbands, the Dana Greeley visit, and the minister-at-large program—contributed to the success of this thriving congregation of more than 200 members.

Portland, Oregon. The West Hills fellowship in Portland, Oregon, has an unusual history that has resulted in its becoming one of the largest lay-led congregations in the UUA. In 1955, a group from First Unitarian Church in Portland, seeking a different kind of religious community, decided to start a lay-led fellowship. By 1962, the fellowship had grown big enough to buy land and acquire a building. Two successive ministers served the congregation over a nine-year period beginning in 1965. The first, Ira Blalock, split his time between First Church and West Hills before becoming full-time at West Hills. He and the fellowship had a cordial parting in 1971. The board then called a full-time minister, even though the majority of the members wanted only part-time ministry. This decision, along with financial problems and other issues, created a difficult situation for the new minister, leading to a termination of that relationship in 1975. At that point the congregation reverted to lay-led status.

As in many other fellowships, the decision not to have a minister was a continuing source of controversy for West Hills. In 1981, Gordon McKeeman served the congregation as a minister-on-loan. Despite a positive experience with McKeeman, a survey of the congregation in May of that year showed a substantial majority opposed to calling a minister at all, with most of the rest wanting only a part-time minister.

From that point on, West Hills remained lay-led. In 2005, the congregation celebrated its 50th anniversary with 157 members, a $125,000 budget, and three paid part-time staff—a volunteer coordinator/administrator, a director of religious education, and a choir director—but no minister.

West Hills has always been focused on religious education (for both children and adults), fine arts, and engagement in social action and public issues. Like many lay-led congregations, it has a variety of special-interest groups and social activities. Mirroring trends in Unitarian Universalism in general, the fellowship's Sunday services have seen a shift in emphasis away from what the congregation's history calls "flinty," or dogmatic, humanism. Today, services incorporate more ritualistic elements such as candles, chalice lightings, joys and sorrows, music, and dance.

It is rare to find a 50-year surviving fellowship that is now a medium-sized congregation but has chosen not to engage full-time professional religious leadership. West Hills's story represents an important piece of the multifaceted diversity that both enriches and challenges Unitarian Universalism as a faith community.

California

As most Americans know, there are in effect two Californias, north and south, each more than big enough in population and land area to be a state in its own right. The two areas are very different from each other in geography, climate, and culture. The Unitarian Universalist Association recognizes the two Californias by dividing the state between two districts. Northern California, along with most of Nevada, is in the Pacific Central district, while the southern half of the state is part of the Pacific Southwest district.

Northern California shares some of the pioneer history of the Pacific Northwest, particularly the gold rush of 1849 and thereafter. The region's tradition of pioneer independence and self-sufficiency is reflected in the particularly strong elements of fellowship culture found in some surviving lay-led fellowships.

Northern California is blessed with one of Unitarian Universalism's two seminaries, Starr King School for the Ministry in Berkeley. The seminary is a great resource for area congregations, especially lay-led fellowships in need of consulting ministers, student and intern ministers, or pulpit supply.

Thomas Starr King, for whom the seminary is named, was an important figure in California history as well as the history of both Unitarianism and Universalism. King moved to San Francisco in 1860 and quickly became involved in the new state's politics. According to General Winfield Scott, the Union Army commander-in-chief, Starr King "saved California to the Union." His statue is found in both Golden Gate Park and the United States Capitol, although at this writing an effort is underway to replace the statue in the Capitol with a more conservative icon.

Starr King School is located in a hotbed of liberal and radical politics and alternative lifestyles. These elements of Bay Area culture create a cutting-edge image for Unitarian Universalist congregations in the region—an image that attracts some newcomers and repels others.

Northern California has 20 surviving first-wave fellowships, a majority of the 37 congregations in that part of the state. Only three of these fellowships—Porterville, Redding, and Visalia—have less than 30 members. Two others have between 30 and 100 members. The rest are midsize congregations, with four having more than 300 members.

Several congregations in this region have been described by district leaders as "stuck"—unable to move forward and resistant to constructive change. Chico, with 52 members, has a determinedly "go it alone" attitude and remains lay-led after some unsuccessful experiences with professional ministry. The Humboldt UU Fellowship in the far northern town of Bayside has spent much more of its existence without a professional minister than with one, and at 189 members is one of the largest first-wave fellowships to have done so. Faced with a financial choice between a building and a minister, the congregation chose the building. It relies on Starr King (despite the great distance) to provide student ministers as pulpit supply and has developed a strong, well-trained cadre of lay leaders.

In the early 1950s, the Berkeley congregation spawned the Mount Diablo fellowship in Walnut Creek, providing a more convenient location for some of its members. Laile Bartlett, who wrote the first history of the fellowship movement, was a member of that congregation until her death in 2006. Religious education was the fellowship's major focus; the adults attended lectures and discussions. The congregation relied on Starr King students and nearby ministers for leadership.

It took ten years for Mount Diablo to call a minister of its own. By then the core leaders wanted a "real church," but they encountered resistance from the anticlerical attitudes so prevalent among first-wave fellowships. Even today, elements of fellowship culture are evident at Mount Diablo, particularly the desire for strong lay leadership and small-group interpersonal relationships. But these needs are being addressed in constructive ways appropriate for a larger (400-member) congregation. David Sammons, minister of the congregation between 1984 and 2006, found that the greatest challenge arising from the congregation's fellowship history was in developing worship and worship leadership.

Today Mount Diablo is a teaching church, repaying the help it received from the Berkeley church and Starr King School in its early years. The church sits on a hilltop, with the sanctuary situated to take advantage of the spectacular view. According to Sammons, this is a congregation that believes that the future of the Unitarian Universalist movement lies in building for our grandchildren, not for ourselves. The emphasis on religious education in its founding has provided the core around which the church attracts and serves all its members.

Starr King was not the only resource for developing Northern

California's many first-wave fellowships. Several congregations, including Santa Rosa, took advantage of the minister-on-loan program. Santa Rosa was also fortunate to have help from the district, as well as a rich pool of retired ministers to draw from for pulpit supply. A downside of having such resources is that the congregation takes much longer to face up to the need, and the expense, of full-time professional ministry.

Southern California is the region of older history and Spanish settlement, of mild climate and inland desert. It is dominated by the sprawling city of Los Angeles but is also home to many other large urban areas. Of the 40 congregations in Southern California, just over half (22) began as fellowships.

Unitarianism was not unknown in this area. Ten congregations in this region predate the fellowship movement, mostly in urban centers like Los Angeles, Pasadena, Long Beach, Riverside, and San Diego. They provided the emerging fellowships with opportunities for support, visiting ministers, and participation in district activities. Fellowships formed an important nucleus of growth for the district, since only a handful of new congregations have emerged in Southern California in the post-fellowship period.

Five of the surviving first-wave fellowships remain very small, with under 50 members. Seven range in size from 60 to 126 members. The remaining ten are midsize congregations of 150 members or more (all with ministers).

The San Dieguito congregation is the largest of the surviving first-wave fellowships. It was established in 1949 as a spin-off from the San Diego church. The congregation met in rented quarters for several years until they were able to occupy their present site on a hillside with an ocean view. After 25 years of lay leadership, the first minister was called in 1984 and served for 15 years. The congregation now has 242 members, professional leadership in both music and religious education and an active social justice program. To the outside observer, San Dieguito looks more like a traditional Unitarian Universalist urban church than the typical fellowship-born congregation.

Orange County offers a similar success story, but with a very different beginning. It is one of the rare congregations that began as a Universalist, rather than Unitarian, fellowship, although it did include Unitarians from nearby Santa Ana. Aided by the Universalist minister in Pasadena, the congregation began meeting in homes and rented spaces, then moved into a building of their own in 1960. The congregation called its first minister in 1965 and now has 233 members.

Hawaii

Hawaii is part of the Pacific Southwest District but has only one congregation, located in Honolulu. The congregation was established as a lay-led fellowship in 1952. It is now a ministered congregation with 150 members. Members called their first minister in 1957, just five years after founding the congregation.

Today

New congregations continue to spring up in the Pacific West. Since 1967, the region has birthed 37 new congregations, many based on the contemporary version of the fellowship model. While Hawaii still has only one congregation, Alaska added two new congregations, both lay-led, in 2002 and 2003. Oregon has added eight, six of which are lay-led. Washington has birthed 11 new congregations, only one of which has a full-time settled minister at this writing. California has added 16 congregations, nine lay-led and seven ministered.

The fellowship movement filled in some of those vast empty spaces separating older, established congregations in California, Washington, and Oregon. It also met the need for a liberal religious presence in scattered settlements, many of them small, throughout the region. Although some congregations have failed to grow and thrive, this region has created more medium-sized and large churches out of fellowship beginnings than any other region in the country.

Brilliant Inspiration or Disastrous Strategy?

At the end of his 1994 sermon on the fellowship movement, Dan O'Neal asked:

> How shall we then describe the fellowship movement? Was it just so much wandering through the wilderness worshiping the Gods of isolated rationality and sterile anti-spirituality? Or was it the triumphant entry into the promised land of religious freedom and the New Jerusalem of unencumbered and liberating reason?

Forty years after the formal end of the fellowship movement, judgments about its success as a growth strategy still run the spectrum from wildly positive to extremely negative. The positive view maintains that the congregations planted as lay-led fellowships between 1948 and 1967 saved Unitarianism from near extinction and converted a regional religious movement into a truly national one. Along with growing the denomination, fellowships brought innovation, vitality, and lay leadership into a religious community greatly in need of fresh air. Laile Bartlett is one of the proponents of this upbeat viewpoint.

At the other end of the spectrum is the view that the fellowship movement spawned small, introverted, even hostile groups that did not want to grow or welcome newcomers, did not identify with the larger denomination, and represented Unitarian Universalism in ways that did not reflect the larger movement's self-understanding.

Neither of these views is completely correct, but both contain some important truth. No one description encompasses the diversity of the first-wave fellowships. But the widely held belief that there are many surviving "garage" or "club" fellowships is a myth. Only one-fifth of surviving first-wave fellowships have 50 members or fewer, and only one-seventh are at the cozy family size of 30 members or fewer. Most of the more than 50,000 Unitarian Universalists whose congregations began in the fellowship movement have the benefit of religious communities that offer a broad range of programs and services, including religious education and at least some part-time ministry.

In 1994, Dan O'Neal interviewed four ministers from formerly lay-led fellowships, along with lay leaders. The lay leaders were generally very enthusiastic about their experiences. The ministers were more ambivalent about whether the fellowship program should have been undertaken at all. In the end, however, both groups concurred that there was more good than harm in the fellowship movement. The respondents noted the vitality that fellowship members infused into the larger movement, particularly theologically—in paganism and feminism, for example. In addition, all organizations need criticism as a defense against idolatry. Fellowships provided this kind of critique of Unitarian Universalism. O'Neal's interviews also surfaced the practical matter of money. This was an affordable growth program, perhaps the only affordable one. Fellowships contributed more money to the AUA than they cost in terms of services.

Freedom, Reason and Tolerance

The common understanding of the merger that created the Unitarian Universalist Association is that two bodies came together. But with lay-led fellowships accounting for almost 40 percent of Unitarian congregations at the time, it might be more accurately viewed as a blending of three partners: Unitarian churches, Universalist churches, and lay-led fellowships from both denominations (including eight from the Universalist side). Like the three wise men in the Christmas story, each partner brought their own unique gifts to the union. At the risk of oversimplifying, one might say that the Unitarians brought the voice of reason, Universalists the blessing of tolerance, and fellowships the gift of freedom. These three qualities were first identified by Earl Morse Wilbur when he wrote his history of Unitarianism. When applied to Unitarian Universalism after the merger, each of them is a blessing that also carries a shadow side.

The shadow side of freedom, the gift of fellowship culture, is anarchy—a lack of order and structure, and the inability to create and sustain a center. Those qualities remain the primary danger facing lay-led fellowships. When each person is free to create his or her own religion, there is no grounding, no common core. Unitarian Universalism is not a religion of "anything goes." When we gather in community on Sunday morning to pass life through the fire of thought, we need to hold up our religious experience and understanding to the test of reason. We need to be encouraged to listen to the voices of others with openness and tolerance.

The shadow side of reason, the hallmark of "church Unitarianism" in the 1950s and 1960s, is that spirituality often gets parked outside the door. In the words of author Joanna Macy, humans are more than brains on a stick. We experience with our emotions, our bodies, in relationship as well as alone. It is too easy to rely only on words and our intellect to process experience, or to turn over responsibility for articulating our faith to professional clergy to explain. When others interpret religion for us, our experience is narrowed. We become consumers rather than participants in the creative process. Excessive reliance on reason needs to be held in check by the freedom to question and the tolerance of other ways of being religious.

Tolerance, the gift of the Universalists, also has a shadow side. Those who tolerate everything stand for nothing. Unitarian Universalists spend a lot of time drawing and redrawing boundaries, knowing that revelation is not sealed. Yet some truths are fixed. The seven Principles of Unitarian Universalism espouse the acceptance of diversity. But they also spell out values that define Unitarian Universalism as a faith tradition—respect for the individual and for the natural environment, a commitment to justice, and a duty to engage in the search for spiritual meaning.

Legacy

Perhaps the greatest gift of the fellowship movement is that it held up a mirror—first to Unitarianism, then to Universalism, and finally to itself. Traditional Unitarianism and Universalism were challenged to reflect on their style of operation and to incorporate some of the positive dimensions of fellowship culture. As a result, Unitarian Universalism today reflects a number of changes that can be credited to (or blamed on) the fellowship movement.

Today's popular small group ministry program, for example, owes some of its ancestry to the culture of intimacy in small fellowships. So does the equally popular concept of shared ministry, which brings laypeople into leadership positions. Highly participatory morning worship services have spread from fellowships to the more traditional Unitarian Universalist churches. Some of these changes were welcomed, others resisted.

Shared Ministry

Rev. Tom Chulak, the St. Lawrence district executive, believes that the fellowship movement's most significant contribution, particularly as it absorbed the experiences of the women's movement, was shared ministry. The old patriarchal model of ministerial authority still held sway in many churches in the UUA and in mainstream Christianity prior to the fellowship movement. The earliest challenge to that model came from the Iowa Sisterhood between 1880 and 1930 (as described in "The Midwest").

Fellowships offered a more direct and lasting challenge to the authoritarian model. Organized with largely humanist leadership, they went to the opposite extreme: no authority, no tradition, no rules—anarchy, or close to it. Fellowships also made room for more women in positions of leadership in the 1960s and 1970s, both as lay leaders and later as clergy. Many of these women brought to their work a style that was neither authoritarian nor anarchic.

Women often adopted a more egalitarian and collaborative approach, which facilitated the emerging pattern of shared ministry. A fellowship could call a minister and still develop lay leaders who would collaborate rather than compete with the clergyperson. In such a setting, the minister became less an authority figure and more a coach, a mentor, a source of empowerment and enrichment for the congregation's ministries. Shared ministry spread from fellowships to more traditional churches and is now the norm in most Unitarian Universalist congregations.

The Twenty-first Century

The fellowship story doesn't end in 1967. Many new lay-led congregations have emerged since the end of the fellowship movement. Each new fellowship that comes into being adds another chapter, and another opportunity to our store of knowledge about what works and what does not.

Of the congregations listed in the 2005 UUA directory, 277—more than one-quarter—were established between 1967 and 2004. Some were sponsored by the UUA, some were supported by neighboring congregations, and others arose independently. Of those 277 congregations, 168 are still relatively small and/or without full-time ministry, although some have consulting or part-time ministers. These new congregations are heavily concentrated in seven states far from Boston: Florida, North Carolina, Texas, Minnesota, California, Oregon, and Washington. Those states are experiencing rapid population growth through in-migration, mainly from other regions of the country.

The birthing and nurturing of new congregations in the twenty-first century is very different from the practice before and during the fellowship movement's two decades. Today the growth strategy of the UUA is in a state of transition and experimentation. Deliberate founding of new congregations with start-up funding and a minister has slowed. The emphasis has shifted from starting new congregations to attracting members to existing congregations, with marketing that makes people aware of the existence of Unitarian Universalism as a liberal religious alternative.

Responsibility for nurturing newly formed congregations now falls mainly on the districts. The growing pains experienced by the first-wave fellowships have provided valuable lessons that are being put to good use. Districts give newly formed congregations much-needed support and direction during their developmental phase. The minimum size for affiliation has been increased to 35 members, enough to offer some promise of survival.

Much more effort now goes into preparing congregations to call their first minister. A consulting ministry (typically quarter-time, or at most half-time) with an experienced minister is a common practice—something of a revival of the old minister-at-large and minister-on-loan programs. Sometimes a congregation begins with an interim minister to prepare itself for a regular settlement to follow. These practices help to mitigate the anticlerical bias of a congregation that has been lay-led for a long time.

Fellowships are also now much more likely to have neighboring congregations to turn to for help and support. This is especially true in the Southeast and some parts of the Intermountain West, where fellowships were once so far apart. Today these regions have many congregations that went through the fellowship process, made the transition to full-church status, and can now lend support to their younger brothers and sisters. In part this support is due to the success of the fellowship movement, which helped to triple the number of congregations. New fellowships may draw some members from nearby congregations that bring their experience of how to "do church" with them. The Church of the Larger Fellowship has also expanded its mission to serve isolated groups with up to 50 members, providing resources for worship and religious education.

The story of the Aiken, South Carolina, congregation is fairly typical of recently created fellowships. It was chartered in 2003, drawing some of its first members from the Augusta, Georgia, congregation about 30 miles to the west. From the beginning, the new fellowship's goal was to become a ministered congregation. Augusta's minister has been supportive, and the members who shifted to Aiken largely for reasons of geographic convenience brought useful skills and experience with them. Within a year of its chartering, the congregation had voted to purchase a building. By 2007 it had grown to 60 members, plus a dozen children in religious education. Aiken participates in district affairs and draws worship leaders from a number of area congregations.

Like Aiken, the lay-led fellowships of today and tomorrow should experience much less bumpy transitions than the pioneers of the fellowship movement. Our movement as a whole has learned from its successes and failures in supporting young congregations as they struggle to reach maturity and find their place in the Unitarian Universalist family.

The fact that Unitarian Universalism is alive and well in the twenty-first century is due in no small part to the fellowship movement. It is a livelier, more vital, more diverse religious movement because of the pioneers who took the faith to new places and created a frontier kind of religion. Just as the frontier in the American West settled into established communities, with a scattering of ghost towns, so likewise did these pioneer settlements. But change took place among the senior partners in Unitarian Universalism as well. The entire movement absorbed some of the empowerment of the laity, modified its forms of worship, experimented with new ways to be in community, and appreciated the value of small communities within the larger whole. Unitarian Universalism today has been not only challenged but also enriched and revitalized by the unique phenomenon of the fellowship movement.

Regional Statistics

The impact of the first-wave fellowships on Unitarian Universalism is remarkable. The statistics on the following pages are organized by the five regions described in this book. They reflect the geographical nuances of the fellowship movement and the proportions of fellowships to total congregations by location. This kind of bird's-eye view allows us to appreciate the legacy of these fellowships by showing the broader implications of the fellowship story.

Northeast Region

The following table provides a statistical overview of the fellowships in the Northeast that were founded between 1948 and 1967 and were still functioning as of 2004. The table shows how many fellowships from this period survive and their relative number compared to all Unitarian Universalist congregations in the region.

See "The Northeast" for a definition of the region, which currently makes up 20 percent of the total U.S. population.

Active UU Congregations in Region as of 2004 (Fellowships and Churches)

Founded before 1948	248
Fellowships founded 1948–1967	65
AUA/UUA-sponsored new starts 1948–1967	7
Founded after 1967	42
Total	362

Surviving Fellowships, Founded 1948–1967

Number	65
Average membership	200
Total membership	12,600
Percentage of all UU congregations in region	18%

By State:

New England (6 states)	9
Delaware	1
District of Columbia	0
Maryland	14
New Jersey	10
New York	17
Pennsylvania	14

Southeast Region

The following table provides a statistical overview of the fellowships in the Southeast that were founded between 1948 and 1967 and were still functioning as of 2004. The table shows how many fellowships from this period survive and their relative number compared to all Unitarian Universalist congregations in the region.

See "The Southeast" for a definition of the region, which currently makes up 22 percent of the total U.S. population.

Active UU Congregations in Region as of 2004 (Fellowships and Churches)

Founded before 1948	18
Fellowships founded 1948–1967	69
AUA/UUA-sponsored new starts 1948–1967	1
Founded after 1967	69
Total	157

Surviving Fellowships, Founded 1948–1967

Number	69
Average membership	167
Total membership	13,000
Percentage of all UU congregations in region	44%

By State:

Alabama	8
Arkansas	4
Florida	19
Georgia	7
Louisiana	5
Mississippi	2
North Carolina	7
South Carolina	4
Tennessee	5
Virginia	8

Midwest Region

The following table provides a statistical overview of the fellowships in the Midwest that were founded between 1948 and 1967 and were still functioning as of 2004. The table shows how many fellowships from this period survive and their relative number compared to all Unitarian Universalist congregations in the region.

See "The Midwest" for a definition of the region, which currently makes up 25 percent of the total U.S. population.

Active UU Congregations in Region as of 2004 (Fellowships and Churches)

Founded before 1948	56
Fellowships founded 1948–1967	69
AUA/UUA-sponsored new starts 1948–1967	1
Founded after 1967	53
Total	179

Surviving Fellowships, Founded 1948–1967

Number	69
Average membership	138
Total membership	9,000
Percentage of all UU congregations in region	39%

By State:

Illinois	11	Minnesota	8
Indiana	6	Nebraska	0
Iowa	3	North Dakota	2
Kansas	4	Ohio	8
Kentucky	3	South Dakota	2
Michigan	6	West Virginia	4
Missouri	4	Wisconsin	8

Southwest and Intermountain West Region

The following table provides a statistical overview of the fellowships in the Southwest and Intermountain West that were founded between 1948 and 1967 and were still functioning as of 2004. The table shows how many fellowships from this period survive and their relative number compared to all Unitarian Universalist congregations in the region.

See "The Southwest and Intermountain West" for a definition of the region, which currently makes up 15 percent of the total U.S. population.

Active UU Congregations in Region as of 2004 (Fellowships and Churches)

Founded before 1948	10
Fellowships founded 1948–1967	52
AUA/UUA-sponsored new starts 1948–1967	2
Founded after 1967	49
Total	113

Surviving Fellowships, Founded 1948–1967

Number	52
Average membership	125
Total membership	6,500
Percentage of all UU congregations in region	46%

By State:

Arizona	4	New Mexico	5
Colorado	7	Oklahoma	3
Idaho	3	Texas	22
Montana	4	Utah	0
Nevada	2	Wyoming	2

Pacific West Region

The following table provides a statistical overview of the fellowships in the Pacific West that were founded between 1948 and 1967 and were still functioning as of 2004. The table shows how many fellowships from this period survive and their relative number compared to all Unitarian Universalist congregations in the region.

See "The Pacific West" for a definition of the region, which currently makes up 16 percent of the total U.S. population.

Active UU Congregations in Region as of 2004 (Fellowships and Churches)

Founded before 1948	24
Fellowships founded 1948–1967	69
AUA/UUA-sponsored new starts 1948–1967	6
Founded after 1967	30
Total	129

Surviving Fellowships, Founded 1948–1967

Number	69
Average membership	145
Total membership	10,000
Percentage of all UU congregations in region	53%

By State:

Alaska	4
California	42
Hawaii	1
Oregon	8
Washington	14

Surviving Fellowships, Founded 1948–1967

A Statistical Comparison Among the Regions

	Northeast	Southeast	Midwest	Southwest and Intermountain West	Pacific West
Number of Congregations	65	69	69	52	69
Avg. Membership of Congregations	200	167	138	125	145
Total Membership	12,600	13,000	9,000	6,500	10,000
Percentage of all UU congregations	18%	44%	39%	46%	53%

Notes

A Growth Strategy for a New Era

p. 3 ...*organization of lay societies in 1793.* Dan O'Neal, "In Fellowship We Trust" (sermon, Unitarian Universalist Fellowship of Sonoma County, California, March 27, 1994); Laile E. Bartlett, *Bright Galaxy* (Boston: Beacon Press, 1960) 37-38.

p. 5 ...*under these limiting conditions?* O'Neal, "In Fellowship We Trust."

p. 6 ...*Church of the Larger Fellowship?* O'Neal, "In Fellowship We Trust."

p. 7 ...*listed in the annual Year Book.* Munroe Husbands, "Growing by Units" (memo, 1949), UUA Archives.

p. 8 ...*except in very promising cities.* Lon Ray Call, memo, October 1946, UUA Archives.

p. 8 ...*starting a new congregation from scratch.* Munroe Husbands, memo to the Department of Extension and Church Maintenance of the American Unitarian Association, 1949, UUA Archives.

p. 9 ...*satisfy all spiritual hunger.* Lisa Schwartz, "The Fellowship Movement: A Search for Our Identity" (sermon, Topeka, Kansas, November 7, 2004).

Many Seedlings Make a Forest

p. 12 ...*Unitarianism has the answer for you.* American Unitarian Association pamphlet, UUA Archives.

p. 12 ...*Service is our Goal.* American Unitarian Association pamphlet, UUA Archives.

p. 16 …*rather than in public places.* American Unitarian Association Fellowship Office, *Unitarian Fellowship Newsletter* 11, no. 3 (March 1959), UUA Archives.

p. 17 …*adapt it to local and individual needs.* Bill Lovely, letter to Munroe Husbands, September 1947, UUA Archives.

p. 18 …*75 children were outside playing in the yard.* Bartlett, *Bright Galaxy,* 102.

p. 18 …*appoint an extension minister in 1997.* www.cuuf.net/history/default.html.

p. 19 …*unless it sponsors a church school.* American Unitarian Association Fellowship Office, "Organizing and Serving Unitarian Fellowships" (pamphlet, 1956), UUA Archives.

p. 20 …*"first-year disillusionment."* Munroe Husbands, memo, December 15, 1955, UUA Archives.

p. 21 …*just over two and a half years.* Bartlett, *Bright Galaxy,* 203–204.

p. 21 …*new to Unitarianism.* Bartlett, *Bright Galaxy,* 6–7.

p. 21 …*what can be 10,000 of these people in fellowships in the near future.* Richard B. Gibbs, memo, December 7, 1955, UUA Archives.

p. 22 …*experienced leadership, and other criteria.* Gibbs, memo to regional directors, December 1, 1957, UUA Archives.

p. 22 … *"graduated" to church status.* Laile E. Bartlett, *Moment of Truth* (Boston: Beacon Press, 1968), 26.

The End of an Experiment

p. 23 …*and 55 that folded.* UUA Extension Department, memo, January 6, 1966, UUA Archives.

p. 24 …*and service the existing ones.* Munroe Husbands, undated memo, UUA Archives.

p. 24 …*so far we have chosen the other route.* Gibbs, "The Philosophy of the Extension Department" (memo, June 1966), UUA Archives.

p. 25 …*But this is our challenge.* Munroe Husbands, Eleventh Annual Fellowship Report, UUA Archives.

p. 26 …*has been transferred to the Executive Vice President.* UUA Extension Department, memo, August 1967, UUA Archives.

p. 27 *...spoke to laymen—and to us all.* Peter Raible, citation for award, 1974, UUA Archives.

p. 27 *...and running a $1 million budget deficit.* Warren Ross, *Funding Justice: The Legacy of the Unitarian Universalist Veatch Program* (Boston: Skinner House Books, 2005), 27–28.

p. 27 *...bail the UUA out of its crisis.* Ross, *Funding Justice,* 28–30. For those unfamiliar with the story of the Veatch Foundation, this book is an excellent resource.

Fellowship Culture

p. 29 *...one must understand fellowship culture.* In addition to the sources cited throughout this chapter, our efforts to define and measure fellowship culture are based on visiting more than 20 congregations, interviewing district executives and current and former UUA staff members, and searching the UUA Archives.

p. 29 *..."an atmosphere of permissiveness and freedom."* Bartlett, *Bright Galaxy*, 52.

p. 30 ... *"I can do it all myself."* Bartlett, *Bright Galaxy*, 118.

p. 30 *...introduced a new vitality into a stagnant faith tradition.* Bartlett, *Bright Galaxy,* xiv.

p. 33 *...the institutionalizing of gradual revolution.* James Luther Adams, "The Indispensable Discipline of Social Responsibility: Voluntary Associations" (address at the University of Padua, 1962), published in *The Journal of Liberal Ministry* 6, no. 2 (1966). Reprinted in *James Luther Adams: The Prophethood of All Believers,* George K. Beach, ed. (Boston: Beacon Press, 1986), 255–263.

p. 35 *...on a table near the entrance door.* Author unknown, letter to Munroe Husbands, undated, UUA Archives.

p. 36 *...an atmosphere of informality prevails.* "Welcome to the Prescott Unitarian Universalist Fellowship," http://www.puuf.net.

p. 37 *...whether the word "sacred" still held any meaning.* O'Neal, "In Fellowship We Trust."

p. 37 *...prime obstacle to his freedom.* Mircea Eliade, *The Sacred and the Profane* (New York: Harvest Books, 1968), quoted in O'Neal, "In Fellowship We Trust."

p. 37 ...*mirror image of the rejected position.* This phenomenon was described by psychologist Carl Jung, who called it "enantiodromia."

p. 37 ...*has shaped it as a religious movement.* O'Neal, "In Fellowship We Trust."

p. 44 ...*a corresponding loss to lay leaders.* This problem was described by Ralph Stutzman, a retired Unitarian Universalist minister who became the first minister to a formerly lay-led fellowship in Huntington, New York, in the 1960s.

Becoming Churches

p. 48 ...*and very low interest rates.* Extension Department memo, May 1958, UUA Archives.

p. 49 ...*no connection to the wider Unitarian movement [other] than in name.* Memo, date and author unknown, UUA Archives.

p. 49 ...*the format and content of the Sunday service.* Gibbs, "Problems in New Churches" (memo, American Unitarian Association Department of Extension, April 1961), UUA Archives.

p. 50 ...*tensions around eventual ministerial leadership.* O'Neal, "In Fellowship We Trust."

p. 50 ...*the culture of strong lay leadership they often encountered.* Royal Cloyd, "Under the Palms: The New Church From a Unitarian Universalist Fellowship," unpublished report to the UUA, December 1962.

p. 52 ...*the perceived threat to established lay leadership.* Munroe Husbands, memo, December 15, 1955, UUA Archives.

p. 53 ...*the key to a successful transition.* Gibbs, "Problems in New Churches."

p. 53 ...*religious education, public relations, and personal counseling.* Bartlett, *Bright Galaxy,* 205–206.

p. 54 ...*and calling a minister.* American Unitarian Association Department of Extension, memo, February 14, 1956, UUA Archives.

p. 54 ...*that showed the greatest promise of becoming churches.* American Unitarian Association Department of Extension, memo, February 14, 1959, UUA Archives.

p. 54 ...*create or reshape the children's religious education program.* American Unitarian Association Fellowship Office, "Summer Student Minister Program" (report, 1953), UUA Archives.

p. 57 ...*only one or two a year.* Margaret L. Beard, "An Evaluation of Discontinued UUA Growth Programs: Extension, New Congregations, and Racial Cultural Diversity Ministry," report to the UUA Department of Congregational Services, November 2005.

p. 58 ...*began as lay-led fellowships.* Cynthia Prescott, personal communication, April 6, 2007.

p. 58 ...*new and not-so-new fellowships.* Munroe Husbands, "Extension and Maintenance Philosophy and Program of the U.U.A. and the Districts" (memo, June 1966), UUA Archives.

p. 58 ...*for a five-year period.* Gibbs, "The Philosophy of the Extension Department."

p. 58 ...*overseeing affiliation and recognition.* Bob Wolley, memo to Joe Barth, November 29, 1967, UUA Archives.

p. 60 ...*including print materials and a web site.* The website of the Church of the Larger Fellowship is http://clf.uua.org.

The Survivors

p. 62 ...*isolated from other congregations and the district.* Munroe Husbands, memo to American Unitarian Association Department of Extension, April 1962, UUA Archives.

p. 62 ...*lost its best leaders early in the process.* Munroe Husbands, "Fellowship Case Histories," (memo to American Unitarian Association Department of Extension, undated, circa 1953), UUA Archives.

The Northeast

p. 67 ...*The Northeast.* In our research for this chapter, we visited with two district executives in person and two by phone, as well as conducting group interviews in four congregations.

The Southeast

p. 75 ...*The Southeast.* Because it is our home region, we were able to explore fellowship history firsthand in three of the districts in the Southeast region: Thomas Jefferson, Florida, and Mid-South, in each case meeting with the district executive and focus groups in several congregations.

p. 80 ...*was able to occupy the property.* Bartlett, *Bright Galaxy,* 189–191.

The Midwest

p. 87 ...*The Midwest.* Much of the information in this chapter was obtained through phone conversations with district executives and ministers, as well as historical resources from the web sites of the districts.

p. 87 ...*and Prairie Star districts.* An excellent historical resource for the Prairie Star district is a volume of essays and congregational histories, *Bring O Past Your Honor,* which can be downloaded from the district's web site: www.psduua.org.

p. 89 ...*by male clergy.* The story of the Iowa Sisterhood is told in Cynthia Grant Tucker's *Prophetic Sisterhood: Liberal Women Ministers of the Frontier, 1880-1930* (Bloomington: Indiana University Press, 1994).

The Southwest and Intermountain West

p. 95 ...*The Southwest and Intermountain West.* We visited the district executives and seven congregations in two of the three districts, Mountain Desert and Southwest. The Stillwater congregation gave us the rare privilege of visiting with founding members from 1947.

The Pacific West

p. 103 ...*The Pacific West.* Our lone trip to this region was to northern California, where we met with Patty Lawrence from Starr King School for the Ministry, interviewed two ministers, and conducted a focus group with the Santa Rosa congregation.

p. 103 ...*Pacific Northwest, Pacific Central, and Pacific Southwest.* This region includes all of the original Pacific Coast Conference of the American Unitarian Association, a district established in 1885. In 1893, the Pacific Northwest Conference spun off as a separate entity, with seven churches in Washington and Oregon. In 1902, a Southern California Conference and Central Area Conference were created, forerunners of the present Pacific Southwest and Pacific Central districts. For a history of the Pacific Northwest district, see Gladys C. Burns, *Our Stories: The Pacific Northwest District of the Unitarian Universalist Association 1962–1978* (Olympia, Washington: Ness Press and Design, 1991), 207–209.

p. 103 ...*well below the U.S. average.* U.S. Census Bureau, *Statistical Abstract of the United States 2004–2005*, 56. The average percentage of the population that belonged to Christian churches in 2000 was 47.2 percent. In California, it was 42.7 percent, but in Alaska it was only 33.6 percent, Oregon 30.1 percent, Hawaii 35.6 percent, and Washington 31.6 percent.

p. 106 ...*joys and sorrows, music, and dance.* West Hills has published an excellent history, *Fifty Years of Fellowship: A History of WHUUF 1955–2005,* from which this account is derived.

p. 107 ...*"saved California to the Union."* Celeste DeRoche and Peter Hughes, "Thomas Starr King," Dictionary of Unitarian and Universalist Biography, (www.uua.org/uuhs/duub).

Brilliant Inspiration or Disastrous Strategy?

p. 111 ...*of unencumbered and liberating reason?* O'Neal, "In Fellowship We Trust."

p. 112 ...*than they cost in terms of services.* O'Neal, "In Fellowship We Trust."

p. 116 ...*as a liberal religious alternative.* Conversation with Tracey Robinson-Harris, director of UUA Congregational Services staff group, August 2006.

Index

Page numbers followed by a *t* indicate tables.